The Women's Co-operative Guild. 1883-1904

THE WOMEN'S CO-OPERATIVE GUILD.

1883-1904.

BY

MARGARET LLEWELYN DAVIES,

GENERAL SECRETARY OF THE WOMEN'S
CO-OPERATIVE GUILD.

PUBLISHED BY THE WOMEN'S CO-OPERATIVE GUILD,
KIRKBY LONSDALE, WESTMORLAND.

1904.

INTRODUCTORY NOTE

ON

THE CO-OPERATIVE MOVEMENT.

THE Co-operative Movement, to which the Women's Co-operative Guild belongs, is an Industrial Democracy, where industry (whether in Stores or in Factories) is carried on by the people for the people.

Industrial Co-operative Societies (Stores) are associations of consumers, retailing and manufacturing articles for their own consumption. There are 1,481 of such Societies in England, Scotland, Ireland, and Wales, with a membership of 1,987,768 men and women. Broadly speaking, any adult may become a member of a Co-operative Society on taking up (usually) a £1 share, which can be paid up by instalments. Interest is paid on capital at from 2½ to 5 per cent, the amount of capital per member being limited by the Industrial and Provident Societies Act, under which Societies are registered, to £200. The net profits, after expenses are paid, are shared by all the members, a varying dividend (average 2s. 6d.) being paid to each member on the amount purchased each quarter. A portion (from $\frac{1}{2}$ to $2\frac{1}{2}$ per cent) of the profits is usually assigned to an Educational Fund, which provides for the education and recreation of the members by means of libraries, lectures, classes, concerts, teas, &c. Many Societies possess fine Co-operative halls and reading-rooms. The members govern the Society at Quarterly Meetings through Boards of Management. Societies undertake nearly every sort of business, the size of buildings and number of departments varying according to the number of members, the largest Societies being at Leeds, Plymouth, and Bolton, with 49,000, 34,000, and 30,000 members respectively. Besides retail trading, Societies carry on many productive departments—boot making, tailoring, &c. In 1899 the value of the goods they produced was £3,900,000, a third of all Co-operative manufactures.

THE ENGLISH CO-OPERATIVE WHOLESALE SOCIETY LIMITED is a federation of 1,133 Societies, and is thus a community of nearly a million and a half men and women, buying and manufacturing for themselves. It is (a) a Wholesale Merchant, importing yearly to the value of £5,780,935, and with sales of over £19,000,000 annually; (b) a Manufacturer (and Agriculturalist) making one-sixth of all the articles it sells to the Stores; (c) a Shipowner, with seven steamers; and (d) a Banker. It has 35 factories, and directs the labour of 13,133 employés. The government is controlled by Quarterly Meetings of delegates representing Co-operative Societies, and is carried out by a Board of Directors.

Introductory Note.

Another association into which Societies are federated, is the CO-OPERATIVE UNION LIMITED. The Union helps in the formation of new Societies, issues model rules for Societies, makes recommendations for educational work, publishes literature, supplies speakers, gives advice on legal questions, and watches and promotes legislation on behalf of Co-operators. It unites Co-operative Societies throughout the country by means of numerous Conferences, and organises the Annual Co-operative Congress, attended by over 1,000 delegates. Its business is carried on by a United Board, composed of representatives from seven Sectional Boards belonging to the seven sections into which Great Britain is divided.

In addition to the above Societies and Federations, there are in the Movement, 146 PROFIT SHARING or CO-PARTNERSHIP SOCIETIES, the ideal of which is for the workmen to partly own the capital and share in the management of the particular workshop.

THE WOMEN'S CO-OPERATIVE GUILD is an organisation of the women connected with Industrial Co-operative Societies. It has 363 branches attached to 272 Societies in England and Wales, and the branches, with a membership of 18,600 women, are federated in the Guild.

CONTENTS.

THE WOMEN'S CO-OPERATIVE GUILD.

1883-1904.

—

CHAPTER I.

THE FIRST TEN YEARS.

"THE Women's League for the spread of Co-operation has begun. All who wish to join should send in their names and addresses to Mrs. Acland, Fyfield Road, Oxford."

These words, in large type, appear in the "Woman's Corner" of the *Co-operative News* on April 13th, 1883; and the following note is found in an early Guild record:—"April 15th. We now number seven."

The Women's Co-operative Guild, as the self-governing body of 18,600 Co-operative women is now called, was born and christened in the "Woman's Corner," of which Mrs. Arthur Dyke Acland was the first editor. At the beginning of the year 1883, a special part of the *Co-operative News* (the organ of the Co-operative movement) was set aside for women. Mrs. Acland opened the first "Woman's Corner" with a lively article, which prepared the soil for the seed which was soon to be dropped into it by a reader named "M. L.," from Woolwich. Mrs. Acland wrote:—

"Men have had it all their own way in the *News* for a long time. It is a grand thing to have this corner all to ourselves, in which we women may open out our minds to each other, and make known our thoughts and wants to one another throughout the length and breadth of the land. . . . What are women urged to do when Co-operative meetings are held? 'Come and *buy*'—that is all. We can be independent members of our Stores, but we are only asked to 'come and *buy*.' . . . Why should we not hold our Co-operative mothers' meetings, when we may bring our work and sit together, one of us reading some Co-operative work aloud, which may afterwards be discussed?"

This appeal brought forth various appreciative and suggestive letters, and on February 10th came a proposal destined to bear much fruit, signed "M. L., Woolwich." After quoting a passage from John Ruskin, about Co-operative workshops for girls, the writer, since well known as Mrs. Mary Lawrenson, says:—

"Now, when our Co-operative Union of Women is fairly established, may we not hope that some of these golden dreams will become realities? If only Mrs. Acland and a few others would form a Central Board, and draw up a plan which we all might follow, mothers' meetings ought to be successful, and I should say meetings especially for young girls would be a great benefit."

Referring a little while afterwards to the above quotation, Mrs. Lawrenson says:—"The idea of the Guild was published in a letter from Woolwich. This would have passed unnoticed but for Mrs. Acland, who at once took the matter up." Practical, helpful, and suggestive as Mrs. Acland always showed herself in the "Woman's Corner," the Woolwich proposal was not likely to fall unnoticed. A letter from her quickly follows. In those early days, when, as she says, she was "bombarded with criticism," she took a cautious line, and deprecated women "imitating or competing with men, pushing themselves into positions which have hitherto been held by men, speaking on platforms, or thrusting themselves on to Management Committees, where they would be liable to be laughing-stocks and stumbling-blocks;" but she ends with the encouraging words: "I thought I might take it upon myself to invite practical suggestions in the 'Woman's Corner' for the formation of a Women's League for the spread of Co-operation—suggestions for its name, its rules, and its objects."

Then it was Mrs. Lawrenson's turn again. She wrote on March 10th with practical suggestions for forming a League, with a Board, Conferences, and subscriptions, and asking Mrs. Acland to be President. Her letter concludes:—"Surely all true men will be only too glad to help us. They will find that by helping us poor women they will benefit themselves, and in time may have cause to be proud of the Women's Co-operative League."

The League may be said to have been finally floated at the Edinburgh Co-operative Congress, in June, 1883. There the membership rose from 14 to 50, a subscription of 6d. was decided on, the formation of local branches suggested, and the first leaflet issued.

Thus did the Guild tree take root, planted and watered by Mrs. Acland and Mrs. Lawrenson. The "old order" has indeed changed in these 21 years. New opportunities create new duties, and these are bound up with hitherto unthought-of rights, to the gain not only of women themselves but of humanity. Is it not a matter for congratulation all round, that one of our members, who became a Poor-Law Guardian, should have been chosen as Chairman of the Infirmary and Lunacy Committee of a very large Poor-Law Union?—that a Guild official—the only woman on the Board—should have been appointed this year (1904) Chairman of the United Board of the Co-operative Union? And was not November 11th, 1903, one of the proudest days in the Guild's history, when a great Free Trade demonstration of women, presided over by the Vice-President of the Guild, was held in the Free Trade Hall, Manchester?

During the first ten years we can trace the beginnings of the Guild machinery, the germs of ideas which have become part of the accepted policy of the Guild; and year by year we find Guild leaders appearing in the "Woman's Corner" as writers, as secretaries of branches, or speakers at conferences.

By the end of 1883, three branches had been formed —Hebden Bridge (Secretary, Mrs. Helliwell), Rochdale (Secretary, Miss Greenwood, daughter of the old Rochdale Pioneer), and Woolwich (Secretary, Mrs. Lawrenson). We can imagine the pleasure and excitement at Hebden Bridge when the branch held its first public tea and meeting in February, 1884, attended by over 200 persons. In the report she read, Mrs. Helliwell says:—

"The number on our books is 60. We have had five monthly meetings. Two papers have been read by members of the League on 'Co-operation, and how to improve it.' Two meetings were taken up in discussing Drapery and other things. Some of them alleged that prices were exceedingly high, while others affirmed that, taking into account the quality, the prices were only reasonable. However, a good number were in favour of cheaper goods to meet the wants of the poorer classes, who were obliged to go elsewhere to get them. A deputation of three members was appointed to see the Drapery Committee, and suggest such alteration as might be necessary for doing a good trade."

As might be expected to take place at gatherings of "purchasers," the prices of goods at the Stores were often under discussion. We also read of a few women attending the quarterly meetings of their Societies, while Plymouth members reported that since their branch started, the Society's monthly meetings were attended by as many women as men. As early as 1884 Mrs. Lawrenson and Mrs. Sheldon were elected on the Educational Committee of the Woolwich Society, but the possibility of sitting on Management Committees had hardly occurred to women yet, although one of the very earliest writers to the "Woman's Corner" (Mrs. Newman, of Norwich) was bold enough to conclude a letter with the remark: "In fact, I think there ought to be women on Store Committees."

The branches very soon began starting clubs of different kinds—Clothing, Outing, Coal, Help-in-need, &c.—and also forming Children's Classes. A little later, successful branches like Burnley and Bolton held large meetings, with lectures on sick-nursing and cookery.

In June, 1884, the first short annual report and balance sheet, printed in the "Woman's Corner," was written by Mrs. Acland, who acted as Secretary for the first year. Six branches were in existence—Hebden

Bridge, 60 members; Rochdale, 42; Woolwich, 43; Norwood, 20; Chelsea, 14; Coventry, 16; making a total membership, including associates, of 235. The balance sheet was as follows :—

	£	s.	d.
Received—Subscriptions and Donations......	3	10	9
Spent—Printing, £1. 5s.; Stamps, 8s. 6d.;			
Paper, 5s.	1	18	6
Balance.................. £1	12	3

When Mrs. Acland resigned the Secretaryship, owing to ill health, in 1884,* the first Central Committee, consisting of Mrs. Acland (President), Miss Greenwood (Vice-President), Miss Shufflebotham (Treasurer), Mrs. Helliwell, Mrs. Lawrenson, Mrs. Benjamin Jones, and Miss Allen (General Secretary), was appointed by correspondence. In this year the name of the League was changed to "Women's Co-operative Guild."

Miss Allen, who was then working under the late Mr. Vansittart Neale, in the Co-operative Union Office, at Manchester, only held office for a year. Mrs. Lawrenson succeeded her in 1885, and was General Secretary for four years.

It is a common observation that distinguished men often have remarkable mothers, and it is interesting to note that in the Guild, many of our most prominent workers were greatly influenced by public-spirited fathers, who were "lovers and friends of mankind." Mrs. Lawrenson's father was a trade unionist and

---

* Mrs. Acland remained nominal Editor of the "Corner" till 1886, when Miss Sharp, of Rugby, who had been acting as Assistant Editor, took the post.

The Late Miss GREENWOOD,
Vice-President (Rochdale).

MRS. M. LAWRENSON
(Woolwich).

The Late
MRS. B. JONES
(Norwood).

MRS. ACLAND, *President.*

MISS SHUFFLEBOTHAM
(now Mrs. Trotman),
Treasurer (Coventry).

MRS. HELLIWELL
(Hebden Bridge).

MISS ALLEN (now Mrs. Redfearn),
General Secretary, Manchester.

FIRST CENTRAL COMMITTEE OF THE WOMEN'S
CO-OPERATIVE GUILD, 1884.

Co-operator, when such names implied high moral qualities. His parents were Lancashire people, but Mr. John Molyneux's life was spent in Woolwich as a printer.* His daughter "Mary," one of 11 children, used to help in the printing office, and remembers how she was sent to collect debts, often waiting in smoky clubrooms by night, till club secretaries found time to settle the printer's bill. From her father and his "earnest-minded friends" Mrs. Lawrenson early learnt, she says, "to ponder the 'why' of poverty and distress, and of injustice and weakness, and to build castles in the air;" and from her own life as a teacher, in many English towns and villages, she gained sad experience of her countrymen's conditions, of the neglect of women's powers, and of the lack of provision for their needs.

In 1868, when the Royal Arsenal Society, at Woolwich, was started, the promoters found a sympathetic printer in Mr. Molyneux, and the printing office became for the Committee-men and others, a regular house of call. When the Society's library opened, Mrs. Lawrenson became a constant reader, and her old dreams, she says, revived, and she asked herself if the Co-operative Society could not be made a social centre of a helpful and enlightening kind to young and old? After marrying, and living in Greenwich for some time, Mrs. Lawrenson returned with her husband and only son to Woolwich, and became a member of the Royal Arsenal

---

* Mrs. Lawrenson relates that it was due to Mr. Molyneux's suggestion, based on his experience of Lancashire Burial Clubs, that the Prudential Assurance Society's system of calling for weekly 1d. payments was instituted.

B

Society. Ideas were continually stirring in her mind as to the part women might take in Co-operation, and found expression, as we have seen, in her letter to the " Woman's Corner." As she truly says, " efforts towards association have a value and importance of their own, when they are initiated by persons whose own experience has impelled them to endeavour to lessen the dangers in the paths of women seekers for daily bread."

Mrs. Lawrenson was a gifted speaker, and much of her time was spent in giving encouraging addresses to the branches already formed or about to form. Many of her views were derived from Ruskin, and she was an earnest admirer of the early Christian Socialists, agreeing with them in the profit-sharing ideal of Co-operation, because she believed that in the joint partnership of capital and labour lay emancipation for the workers. Her master in Co-operation was the late Mr. Vansittart Neale, who wrote to her in 1886, as follows :—

Central Co-operative Board,
September 28th, 1886.

MY DEAR MRS. LAWRENSON,

I was much pleased to be able to do anything to further the action of an institution so valuable as the Women's Guild actually is—still more as it promises to be.

You rightly appreciate the functions of Co-operation in my judgment in speaking of it as a "gospel"—the song of peace on earth and goodwill to mankind, and it must be regarded not as a substitute for the ancient Gospel, but as the *complement* of it, the application of it to mould from circumstances of men lives of the spirit, in which consists their internal happiness. The fact that men can make a heaven for themselves within, even under the most adverse outward circumstances, has blinded the eyes even of good men in a great degree to the possibility of creating for all men outward circumstances which shall be the true expression of this spirit, which produces this inward heaven, and the enormous influence these circumstances will exercise on the characters of those who live under them.

I trust that the Women's Guild will do much to foster the dispositions out of which this higher state will arise, and without which it never can arise.

Yours very truly,

E. VANSITTART NEALE.

Mrs. Lawrenson's hopes for the Guild were very high, and they turned largely on what it might do for young girls and children. Besides helping women to a knowledge of Co-operation, and giving opportunities for pleasant social intercourse, she considered that the Guild should promote Co-operative workshops for girls and Co-operative and kindergarten training for children. She was ready to associate herself with general Co-operative work, as is seen by her being elected to the Woolwich Educational Committee and being sent (with Miss Allen and Miss Webb) as a delegate to the Oldham Co-operative Congress in 1885. During her term of office, the number of branches increased to over 50, and the foundations of the present organisation of the Guild were laid. General rules and model branch rules were drawn up, conferences were held, and districts formed, after plenty of outspoken differences of opinion. The question of the character of the annual meetings (held at the time of the Co-operative Congresses) also came up for discussion. Miss Holyoake* (now Mrs. Holyoake Marsh, daughter of the veteran Co-operator, G. J. Holyoake) came forward

---

*Miss Holyoake sat for four years on the Central Committee of the Guild. She was then Secretary of the Women's Trade Union League.

in 1888 with the bold idea that possibly some day the Guild might hold a Congress of its own. She said :—

"Each Guild might send a delegate to a separate Women's Congress, and elect a President to deliver an inaugural address. Many distinguished ladies are friendly to Co-operative objects. If there comes to be a Ladies' Congress, they will no doubt invite M.P.'s to preside, many of whom are favourable to women taking part in public affairs."*

Recognition of the Guild in the movement began to show itself in various ways—the Co-operative Union (in 1886) instituted its yearly grant of £10†—which has since risen to £200—and the women's help was sought by different bodies.

In 1886, a special appeal was made to the Guild, by the Southern Educational Council, to take up the question of Children's Classes. Some work of this kind has always been carried on by Guild members; but the best contribution the Guild can make to the education of children in Co-operation, is in educating the mothers, when the children would learn in a natural, practical manner. It may not be inappropriate here to quote the following passage from the late F. D. Maurice, one of the Christian Socialist band, and one of the early supporters of women's education :—

"Those who think most earnestly of infant education must think of adult education. They must, above all, desire that the mothers should have wise, loyal, English hearts. By all means let us labour for that end. If I did not believe that the education

---

* During the 13 years the Guild has held Congresses, the "distinguished ladies" who have acted as Presidents, have never been other than its own working Presidents.

† The proposal to ask for a grant, as well as to incorporate the Guild Report with the Co-operative Union's Report, came from Mrs. Carter, of Reading, a member of the Central Committee.

of working men would lead us by the most direct road to the education of working women I should care much less about it. But I am sure that the earnest, thoughtful man, who is also a labourer with his hands, instead of grudging his wife the best culture she can obtain, will demand that she should have it. He will long to have a true household; he will desire to bring up brave citizens. He will understand that his country looks to the wives and mothers in every one of her classes as the best security that the next generation of Englishmen shall not make her ashamed."

As the men of the movement gradually came to see that the Guild could be a valuable auxiliary, so the women gradually awoke to their powers. In the South, the women were more easily and quickly accepted as fellow-workers, and such an expression as "Let my wife stay at home and wash my moleskin trousers" would not have been heard at a Southern Conference. But good friends were also found in the North among the men, and it must be confessed that the women have often had themselves to blame for their own "backwardness in coming forward." Writing in 1886, the Secretary of the Norwich Branch says :—" It has been my painful experience in asking mothers to come out for an hour or two to enjoy themselves, they nearly all make one answer—'Oh, thank you! but I never go out, but my daughter will come, or my husband and children will come.'"

But signs of independence and desire to advance were not wanting among the women. A very refreshing article appeared in the "Woman's Corner" from "Mary," protesting against the usual view of women's influence and the pampering of husbands, pointing out the hardness of women's lives and the

need of an equal give-and-take kind of companionship..
And "A Member of the Guild" wrote in March, 1885 :—

"The men must leave home for work, but after working hours
they can attend all sorts of social and political meetings, but if
the women wish for a little variety, and would like to meet
together for a little social intercourse, we are sometimes told we
had 'better attend to our home affairs and keep the stockings
mended.' Now, I believe most women are about as fond of
mending stockings as men are of cleaning shoes. . . . I know
Mr. Acland and Mr. Jones, in their excellent little book 'Working-
men Co-operators,' try and please us by telling us we have all
the advantages in our Societies which are enjoyed by the men,
but it only seems to be so in theory; and if the members of our
Societies are really the cream of the population (as they are said
to be) whatever must the skim-milk class of Englishmen be?"

This writer would have been a keen supporter of
the "Open Membership" campaign the Guild is now
carrying on (see page 100).

One of those who, during this period of progress,
was foremost in work, was the late Mrs. Benjamin
Jones. She was a "Lancashire lass," brought up
amongst mill-workers, and going herself to the mill
every morning, at six o'clock. Her marriage with Mr.
Benjamin Jones brought her into close touch with the
Co-operative movement, of which she soon became an
active advocate. Small, gentle, daintily dressed, she was
at the same time very independent in her views and
actions, and did not shrink from anything that she felt
would benefit her fellows. We trace through the pages
of the "Woman's Corner" how fearlessly she stepped
out along new paths, welcoming fresh ideas, urging
developments in the Guild, speaking with refinement,
humour, and practical sense.

Living at Norwood when the Guild was started, she became Secretary of the Norwood Branch, which was one of the first six, in 1884. She read a paper entitled, " Can Women help the Progress of Co-operation? " at its first meeting.

Mrs. Jones raised the question of speaking from public platforms, as early as 1885. After the line laid down at the Edinburgh meeting, 1884, that there should be "no platform speaking, no advertising, no going out of our woman's place," it required some courage to bring the subject up at the Guild meeting at the Oldham Conference (1885). Writing to the "Corner," she says :—

"This was a matter of great importance to me (public platform speaking), myself being the first of the Guild in taking that step. The Guild of Co-operators have cordially invited women to assist them in the spread of Co-operation round London. As this cannot be done by staying at home, if, when accompanying our husbands to a meeting, we are invited to address a few words to the women, we should do our best. I am told it is unwomanly, but, having carefully thought this matter over, I decided to bring it before our meeting at Congress. As the Women's Guild is growing rapidly, and requires more earnest work, I should not like to do anything in connection with it which would be likely to deteriorate us in the eyes of our fellow-workers . . . Many of those present spoke up and said they did not disapprove of speaking from platforms, and we ought not to be afraid to do anything that would help to bring the women more forward, and encourage them to form branches of the Guild at every Store."

Mrs. Jones was elected on the first Central Committee, and when Mrs. Acland gave up the Presidency, Mrs. Jones held the post for five years, from 1886 to 1891, returning to the Central Committee for 1893, until her death in May, 1894. During these years she was full of ideas and of active work. At the Guild meetings during the Congresses of 1885 (Oldham), 1886 (Plymouth, where there was a great advance, the meeting being attended by 300 persons), and 1887 (Dewsbury), Mrs. Jones read papers on "Guild Children," "Drapery Departments," and "The Formation of a Southern District Committee." She was the first to suggest that conferences should be held and districts should be formed. The following passages from her speeches and writings show her sympathy and freedom from prejudice, and how true her instinct was in different directions :—

"They had that morning been listening to the Congress paper, 'How to bring Co-operation within reach of the Poorest,' and she thought if anyone in connection with Co-operation could take a step in that direction it was the Women's Guild. . . . One step she hoped to see taken before very long was that where there was a poor neighbourhood they should open a Store in the district, and do their very best to promote the good of the people by visiting them and taking an interest in their welfare."—*Report of speech at Guild Meeting at Lincoln Congress, 1890.*

"I believe women would be found of great use on School Boards, Vestries, and as Poor-law Guardians."

"Mothers should try to keep up their education so that their children should not be ashamed of them."

"It was not uncommon that a buyer in London would ask for 2oz. of tea or one pennyworth of starch. It was this poorest class that the Guild ought to try and get hold of and help by means of Co-operation."

"She welcomed the prospect of women becoming members of Committees. . . . It did good that women should take their part in everything, and the Guild, as an association of women, should take up all the subjects with which women were concerned. . . . Many men could not understand a balance sheet, and it was a thing which women could learn. They should remember that at least they could not make greater blunders than men had done."

MISS LLEWELYN DAVIES,
General Secretary

From this short account of Mrs. Jones' work, our readers will see how great a loss the Guild sustained when she died, in her 46th year, in 1894. Of her family life this is not the place to speak, more than to say that her gentle, lovable nature made her more than usually loved by husband, and children, and friends. Mr. Jones, in a letter thanking the Central Committee for their sympathy, said, "It is a great consolation to our children and to me, that she succeeded so well in making our home an earthly paradise, while at the same time she was able to do so much to promote the happiness of others." The following year the "Mrs. Jones Guild Convalescent Fund" was started in memory of her. (See Chapter VI., page 104.)

Another supporter of women's rights and duties was Miss Tournier, of Chelsea, who worked ardently for the Guild, first as Southern Sectional Secretary (1889), then as Vice-President and as President (1891 and 1892), until severe illness, from which she has never wholly recovered, enforced her retirement from work. Her glowing enthusiasm and rousing speeches made her much sought for as a speaker, and she has earned the gratitude of all who knew her, not only for her whole-hearted labour for the Guild when she was occupied in teaching, but also for the patience, hope, and unfailing interest she has shown during many weary years of confinement.

In 1889, Mrs. Lawrenson resigned her post of General Secretary, and her place was taken by the present writer, who gained her first Co-operative experience among the

Co-operators of Marylebone. Her home that year was removed from London to Kirkby Lonsdale, Westmorland, so that the headquarters of the Guild had also to be changed from the South to the North of England.

Of the 50 branches of the Guild in existence in 1889, only seven were in the North. The immense growth of the Guild in Lancashire and Yorkshire, destined to occur as soon as the idea took root among the mill-workers, will be seen in these pages.

One of the most honoured names in the Guild annals of the North comes into prominence this year, that of Miss Reddish, of Bolton. She read a paper on "Guild Work" at the first conference held in the North, at Bolton, where she has been President of the Branch for 15 years, from 1886 to 1901. We cannot but offer her here a slight tribute of affection and admiration for her character and untiring work in the Co-operative and Labour movements.

She left school at 11, and began work at home as a little girl, winding silk on a frame with 12 pegs, becoming, as it was termed, a "disciple of the apostles"—preparing the silk for weaving, which her mother and the neighbours wove on their hand-looms. Later on, she entered the mill, working as a "winder" and "reeler" at a cotton spinning mill. Then she became a "roller-coverer," where her duty was also to render "first aid" in the painful machinery accidents which often occurred. Afterwards she was forewoman in a hosiery mill, thus gaining

Miss Reddish (Bolton).

an intimate knowledge of the lives and needs of the workers. She brought a mind full of reasonableness and sympathy, and an unusual strength of feeling for justice and truth, to bear on her experiences of industrial life, and her aspirations reached out towards what is known as a socialist form of society. In one of her addresses she says :—

"I believe that all the physical, social, and moral evils have their source for the most part in a bad economic and industrial system, and, therefore, I would have society and the industry of the kingdom established and worked on new lines—on the lines of true and universal Co-operation, or the principle of equal efforts in producing and equal participation in results. I would have no superior recognised but the superior in intelligence, morals, and honour, which should be based on commendable service to all. . . . The first and highest duty I would have taught in schools is the sacred duty of each to labour for and promote the highest good of society, and that of society to promote the highest good of each individual comprising it. . . . When we have used our best efforts to bring about this great and desired end of universal Co-operation we shall feel that we have done our duty to our fellows in the endeavour to realise the hopes and wishes of the great founders of the Co-operative movement, that poverty and idleness should disappear from the land; that idleness should cease to revel in luxury and labour pine in want; that vice should no longer glitter in the palace and virtue droop in the hovel; that man's inhumanity to man be a thing only of the past. Let us all do our best to bring about that possible condition of life wherein virtue and justice and love are with and for all, and the beautiful dream of universal brotherhood shall become a lasting and grand reality."

It was in 1889, that Miss Reddish gained a seat on the Central Committee. In 1893 she became Guild Organiser for two years, and since that time has never ceased to be connected with the Guild in varying ways, working always for the allied causes of women and labour.[*]

This year (1889) showed considerable advance in the general organisation of the Guild. The branches were grouped under six District Secretaries (all in the South), and two Sectional Secretaries (for South and Midlands) were appointed. The first " Winter Circular," containing a list of lecturers, and recommending an examination in chapters of the " Laws of Every Day Life," was issued; the Annual Report was printed in book form, for which a diminutive schedule of questions had been sent to Branches; and two Sectional (in North-West and South) and three District Conferences were held.

As the Guild grew, courage increased. It was urged that the Guild meetings were different from " mothers' meetings," that women had public duties of every kind—that the Store was a training ground for citizenship for women as well as men—that the members of the Guild were a body of reformers, whose influence must be exerted in the solution of the labour question.

This period may fittingly close with the greatest event which had so far taken place in the history of the Guild, namely, the *Festival at Manchester to celebrate the formation of 100 Branches in the Guild,*

[*] Miss Reddish stood for the Bolton School Board in 1897. She was defeated, but when in 1899 a vacancy occurred, it was expected that she would be co-opted to fill it, as it was usual to select the highest defeated candidate. But the Board departed from this custom, simply on the ground that she was a woman. At the regular election a few months later, the electors took a different view, and she was returned. It is of interest to find that in 1870, when the first School Board was nominated in Bolton, Miss Reddish's father spoke strongly in favour of women being elected on to School Boards.

in July, 1892. The Festival lasted three days, two days being devoted to the various Presidents' addresses and to papers and discussions. Seventy-seven branches were represented by 120 delegates, and many visitors of interest were present. A special fund of £120 was raised, and expenses of one delegate from each branch paid. How interesting an occasion this was to the delegates, some of whom had never left home for eight, twelve, and even eighteen years, may be imagined. "The older women specially," wrote a member afterwards, "had had no outings of the kind, having experienced only 'mothers' meetings' and treats; but this affair seemed

MISS WEBB.

to show them they were of importance, and some of the older women marvelled at it."

Full reports of the Festival were given in the *Co-operative News*. The Chairmen of the meetings were Miss Tournier, the late Mrs. B. Jones, Mrs. Acland, and Miss Reddish. Among the readers of the five papers * was Miss Catherine Webb, whose father was a Director of the Co-operative Wholesale Society, and whose family were long connected with the Co-operative Society in Battersea.

* (1) "The Guild and Store Life," by Miss Webb; (2) "A National Alliance," by Miss C. Black, then Secretary of the Women's Trade Union Association; (3) "Co-operative Productions and the Needs of Labour," by Mrs. Vaughan Nash; (4) "Women and Municipal Life," by Mrs. Knott, of Parkgate; and (5) "Future Guild Work," by Miss Spooner, then, as now, Secretary of the Southern Section.

C

Miss Webb is an expert in Co-operation. She was trained in all the business side of the movement, and is versed in balance sheets and the work of Committees and employés. Miss Webb was an early member of the Central Committee, and was the second woman to sit on the Southern Sectional Board of the Co-operative Union. She has also contributed much to the literature of the Guild, being constantly connected with the "Woman's Corner,*" and the writer of many pamphlets. She wrote a short account of the first ten years of the Guild in 1894, and has recently edited a text book on the Co-operative Movement.

The Manchester Festival gave a great impetus to the Guild. The "Winter Circular," issued in September, 1892, says :—" Never, we think, has the Guild outlook been more hopeful. The number of our branches (100) and members (4,050) is larger than it has ever been; the wheels of our organisation are beginning to move easily and efficiently ; our financial position has much improved, the Union grant being increased to £50; and there is a conscious feeling growing up of progress and power, showing that the Guild is rapidly becoming a movement full of force and life."

---

* During the last few months Miss Webb has been temporarily editing th₃ "Woman's Corner."

CHAPTER II.

A DEMOCRACY OF WORKING WOMEN.

THE principle underlying the whole organisation of the Guild, from top to bottom, is that of *self-government*. This characteristic is much valued by the members, on account of the training and sense of comradeship it gives. "The great point to me," says a Lancashire mother, formerly a mill-worker, "is that we are so democratic; no patronage, but all to take their share in the government." And the same thing strikes an engineer's wife in the South—"The one great difference between the Guild and other bodies of women I have come in contact with is, may I say, its splendid democracy. The humblest member can feel that she stands on an absolute equality with the most lofty." Other members say: "We have none of the so-called 'upper ten' ruling us." "It brings us more on a level with one another. If in a Guild Branch there were any feeling 'I'm above you,' then I think it would spoil the harmony of a Branch at once; and a person that took that line would get marked up." While in Lancashire dialect the same idea comes out as follows: "Guild isn't like most other things. After yun bin a member three months, yur can take ony position as mi be oppen, *if,* and that's a little word, but it means a greight deal, if yur other members think yur fit for't."

The Guild is composed of 363 *Branches*, varying in membership from 10 to 700 women, connected with industrial Co-operative Societies; branches are associated together into 34 *Districts*, and also into five larger groups called *Sections*. These are all governed by Committees elected from their special constituencies, while the whole Guild is ruled by its Annual Congress, through a Central Committee of seven, elected by all the branches.

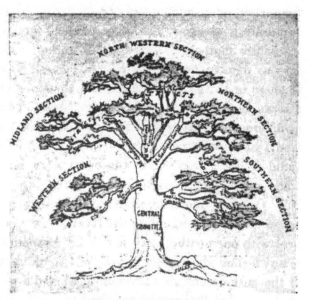

WOMEN'S CO-OPERATIVE GUILD.

The object aimed at in this organisation is healthy independence in local work, combined with response to the policy and suggestions coming from the centre. That a satisfactory understanding exists is shown in various ways—in the loyal support of the Branches, in the prompt payment of branch subscriptions, and in the return, in less than three weeks, of 360 forms containing information for the annual report—those " dreadful scheddles," as they have been termed. The other day it was reported that a Co-operator in the Midlands greatly admired the Guild organisation. " Why," he said, " touch it at any point, and it's known at the Central."

A venerable American temperance worker was once heard to say that heaven was spoken about as a place where there were no partings—but as for her, she hoped it would be a place where there were no *meetings*. Certainly no age has ever been so given over to meetings as our own, and Co-operative women are as good "meetingers" as the rest of mankind. Branches, districts, and sections, and the whole Guild, do their work by means of meetings, conferences, and congresses respectively, the means being supplied in each case by special funds.*

At the time when the Guild was started, the only regular meetings which working women used to attend

---

* (a) *Branch Funds.*—These are obtained by the subscriptions paid by the members,. varying from 6d. to 2s. a year, most commonly 1s. a year; 141 branches receive in addition annual grants from their Societies or Educational Committees, varying from £1 to £40 a year. (b) *District Funds.*—These are raised by a subscription from the branches in the district, usually of 2d. per member annually. Where more funds are needed grants are given from the Central Fund. (c) *Sectional Work.*—Special grants are made from the Central Fund to the Sectional Secretaries. (d) *Central Fund.*—This is raised by a subscription of 2d. per member from all the branches, with the addition of a grant of £200 from the Co-operative Union. A special annual Congress Fund is raised each year, for which a substantial grant is relied on from the inviting Society, the remainder being raised by donations kindly given by other Societies in the section.

were of a religious or philanthropic character—
"mothers' meetings"—where the promoters might be
described as working *for* and not *with* the people, and
where no ideas of working women's rights and wrongs
or of their citizenship, ever crept in.   The difference
between a Guild and "mothers'" meeting was described
by one of our members as follows :—

"One is democratic, the other autocratic. While the one
strives to educate its members in the broadest sense of the word,
and encourages its members to take part in Co-operative and
social reform, the other ('mothers' meeting') tends rather to
keep its members' views narrow, to concentrate their whole
attention on Church matters, and not to launch out and take part
in the political and social reforms which are necessary if we wish
to get out of the quagmire of humdrumness."

"I used," said another member, "to attend a
mothers' meeting, and did so more from a point of
duty than anything, but after joining the Guild I did
not feel to have patience to listen to the simple, childish
tales that were read at the former, and did not like to
feel we had no voice in its control."   Over and over
again, members speak of the variety of subjects taken
up in the Guild as distinguishing it from other societies,
and the enlightening and broadening effect it has on
them.

BRANCHES.

The size of the Branches, and the quality of their
work, vary considerably. There are always a few in
low water, but the general prosperity is much greater
than it used to be. Lack of sympathy and financial
support from their Societies is perhaps the chief cause
of weakness, but in some places, it is very difficult to

interest the women in Guild work. Every year some Branches—on an average about 12—die out altogether.*

Branch meetings are usually held on Co-operative premises, sometimes in hired rooms. But the only place available may be a loft, with flour bags to sit on. We get such contrasts as these in letters from Branch Secretaries:—From S.: "We have only a very small room to meet in. If there are twenty in it we are too crowded to move, so you will see we have no convenience for lectures or anything else." From B.: "We have got a nice room—fine, and all up to date—and we are enjoying ourselves. We have got 91 members, and keep getting two or three more every week."

If we paid a visit to one of our large North-Western branches, say at Darwen or Accrington, where the grants from the Societies are at least £40 a year, we should see a company of women in a fine Co-operative Hall over the Store, presided over by one of their number on the platform, the Secretary seated by her side, with minute book on the table. Business will be first disposed of; for example, correspondence from the General Secretary, suggesting an anti-credit campaign or a Factory Bill resolution; the election of delegates to a conference or congress; arrangements for an excursion over a Co-operative Factory, or with the Educational Committee for a Christmas or summer treat for members' children. Then may follow a

---

* Roughly, in the last 15 years, Branches connected with 100 Societies have broken up entirely. In addition, about 80 Branches have died and started again, while about 80 others have become extinct owing to the break-up of their Societies.

lantern lecture on the Guild, Co-operative productions or "The White Slaves of England," or a visit from one of the Guild officials, or a County Council lecture on sick-nursing, or an address from a Committee-man of the Store on the balance sheet, or from a Poor-Law Guardian, or the Secretary of a Woman's Suffrage Society. Or the subject for the evening may consist of a paper on Co-operation or the Guild, by a local member, followed by discussion. For one of the points kept in view is the bringing out and training of individuals, so as to fill the official ranks with the best officers. Public speaking for conferences and propaganda work is, of course, most necessary for Guild progress, and visitors to our meetings are often surprised to see the ready, practical, humorous, and sometimes eloquent speakers that the Guild produces. "Our Guild," says a member, "has turned out women who are capable of making speeches such as few men could beat—women who all their lives have worked hard in the factory and the home." To further encourage all those who are most intelligent and aspiring, special individual education is provided for by means of correspondence classes, reading parties, essay competitions, and examination questions.

The friendliness and sense of brotherhood so much a part of the Co-operative creed, is encouraged by the various teas, social evenings, and coffee suppers, which always form a part of branch work.

Many remarks could be quoted as to the way the meetings are appreciated, e.g.: "You would be pleased to see the interest our members take in our meetings.

Last Wednesday I never expected seeing more than a dozen, it was such a bad night; but would you believe it, there were 30 present." "As soon as I wake on Thursday morning I think, 'Oh, it's Guild day, I must get on, for I would sooner go without my dinner than miss the Guild.'" One of our newest Secretaries writes, "We have made a glorious start, and I feel confident the women would do anything rather than miss our Guild evening."

This is how Northumberland Guildswomen speak of the meetings:—"The Guild night is my rest. Ah hed been weshin arl day, an was hurring to get ready. Wor man says, 'Ye better sit yorsell down an get a rest.' Ah says, 'No, ah rest at th' Guild, an hear somethin gud inta the bargain.'" Another says, "Ah niver thout there was onything in Co-operation for women except divi, now ah's always sure to hear somethin fresh at th' Guild." And another, "Ah have been bad arl day, but ah knew if ah could get to th' Guild ah shood be a bit lot better."

A cause that contributed much to the progress of the Guild, to the increase in branches, and the improving quality of their work, was the fact that for nearly eight years we were able to employ a special "Organiser." * Miss Reddish held the post for two years (1893-5), and she was followed by Miss Mayo (of Huddersfield), who in every variety of weather, wearying journeys, and

---

* An Organiser's Fund was established, as the Guild funds were insufficient for such an expense. Miss Ada Mocatta, who has been a constant friend of the Guild for nearly twenty years, was a contributor to this fund. She took the present writer's place as Secretary of the Marylebone Branch for some years.

varying fortunes and misfortunes, kept with splendid perseverance to the work for between five and six years.

When a Branch of the Guild was formed at Berry Brow, Huddersfield, where Miss Mayo was living, she

Miss Mayo.

became its Secretary, and since then has been Organiser and Council Member.

The whole Guild owes much to her bright cheeriness and true feeling of comradeship, which must often have been of service to her, for, in spite of the extreme kindness and hospitality of Co-operators, a lecturer's life is sometimes not a happy one. She says:—

"Once upon a time I was drawn by a pony, I hardly think it could have been a Co-operative one, that ambled at the pace of a goat, taking over an hour and a half for six miles, and that insisted on stopping at each public-house we passed. Wet driving snow was falling, and on arriving at the station I looked like Lot's wife; from the shawl over my head to my feet I was white. Before I could thaw or scrape the snow off, my train came up, and I had several hours' journey to the next meeting, after which I was nursing a cold for a fortnight."

"Another day, while trudging two miles from tram to meeting one dark winter's night, and while being guided across a ploughed field by way of a short cut, the bottom came out of the slide box, and all the slides slithered down among the furrows. Whenever I miss one, I always think it must have been lost then."

And here is another experience :—

"On visiting a town to speak at a branch in a new locality on its outskirts, I took the tram bearing the name of the suburb, and I alighted at the terminus in a dark residential quarter. When I asked for the Store it was pointed out to me in the distance, on the other side of a large sheet of water. The floods were out, and I ought to have taken a tram to the further and higher side, but no one had thought of mentioning it. It was late, and there was not time to go all the way back again. There were no cabs, and the nearest stand was a mile away. The water appeared to be six or eight inches deep; piles of stones, sticks, and a shed or two, and other signs of building, stood out of it. I inquired for a cart, but they had all gone away for the night. At last, after much persuasion, a coke merchant at the corner of the street was induced to lend his coster's cart. A pony was produced from an outhouse, an orange box put up for me to sit on, and then, clasping my slides tightly, we started. It was just like going out to sea in a bathing machine. We bumped and splashed over stones and into holes, but at last arrived, and found all the audience on the pavement watching my progress with excitement, and wondering why I had chosen that route."

DISTRICTS AND SECTIONS.

We have seen in Chapter I. how, as the branches grew in numbers, the need for more official workers was felt, and also for intercourse and united work among the branches. So, first, we find District Secretaries being appointed, till, through various developments, we have our districts, with their own elected Committees, special rules (based on model district rules drawn up by the Central Committee), and funds. District Committees form a useful training ground for our members. The duties of a Committee are to start new branches, visit old ones, and plan out and carry through District Conferences, which bring the members together on easy and helpful terms.

SECTIONS.

Working in close touch with the districts, come some of the most important officials in the Guild—the Sectional Secretaries—the guides, philosophers, and friends of the branches and districts. In connection with them, and meeting half-yearly in each of the sections (North-Western, Midland, Northern, Southern, and South-Western and Western), the Sectional Councils work.

The great events in the sections are the conferences which take place, in each, twice a year. These are held in large Co-operative Halls, and are attended by from 100 to 300 delegates and members, and representative men from various boards and bodies in the movement. Many of the delegates arrive before the conference hour (3 p.m.), so as to visit the Co-operative Store and town and see all they can on their "day out," having often got up at 4 or 5 a.m. to do the day's washing or baking. On entering the hall there is an air of expectancy; hearty welcomes are received by the better known officials, new branch delegates are introduced, and members exchange news of their work. An invariable feature is a stall of Guild leaflets of all kinds, the majority of which are sold at 1d. Business begins with a few words of welcome from the inviting branch, and a short, stirring address from the Chairman. Next follows the Sectional Secretary, with her year's report, if the conference is in the spring, and then the subject for the afternoon is opened by the reader of the paper.

It is the usual custom to take the same subject at each of the Sectional Conferences, which is fixed by the Central Committee. It generally has reference to some question which is affecting the Guild or the Co-operative movement at the time, e.g., Co-operative Old Age Pensions,* Co-operative Education, Co-opera-tion and the Poor, &c., or to some municipal or national question indirectly affecting Co-operators and the movement, e.g., Women's Suffrage, Condition of Women Workers, the Land Question, Free Trade, &c.

At the close of the conference a lively tea party takes place, while the Sectional Secretary makes the

---

* The subject of Co-operative Pensions has once or twice been considered by the movement. Guild women have decided against Co-operative Pensions, and declared "That a national scheme is the only satisfactory solution of old-age poverty." A paper on the subject was read by Miss L. Harris (Assistant Secretary) at the five Sectional Conferences in 1901, which made quite clear that the majority of Co-operators could not afford to save for old-age pensions, that the purchasing qualification proposed by the scheme put forward by the United Board was impossible, that a pension scheme would act as a check on Co-operative developments, and, finally, urged that Co-operators should support a scheme of national pensions.

regulated payments of half fares to one delegate from each branch.

Old members are often amused at the remarks new delegates make, after attending their first conference— "My word, I never thought that women could speak on such subjects. I say, how do they manage to learn?" or, "This has been an eye-opener to me! Ah never thought that women could talk out but gossip before to-day, but I tell yo', some on 'em can shame men i' talking common-sense."

The interest continues when the conferences are over, as may be gathered from the following incident, described by a member:—

"Eh! Awst never furget once coming fro' Manchester. Wha bin having a Sectional Conferance there. Eight of us ut lived in one direction agreed to go back bi't' same train. Nimblest and leetest, of course, geet to th' train fust, un took their seats in an empty carriage. Then in popt a chap none of 'em knew. Th' heavy weights come puffing up soon after, just on t' last minuet. Ough't lot geet together. Th' train started, un so did our tungs, talking about what wha had sin an' yerd. Th' chap seemed to be reading a paper. After a while he axt ur pardon, un said he'd bin deeply interested in ur talk, un fro' what he could make out we were all interested in sommut ut whur for t' general good, un as he knowd good work couldn't be done wi'out good brass, if we would accept hauve-a-crown he'd be glad to give it to us. Aw con tell yo' wha did accept it wi' thanks, and handed it o'er to our District Treasurer."

The largest sections in point of numbers, and the most active, are the North-Western and the Southern, where the two Secretaries, Miss Bamford* and Miss Spooner, have been re-elected year after year for 10

---

* While these pages were being written Miss Bamford's name has changed to that of Mrs. Tomlinson.

and 13 years respectively.   When Miss Bamford first
took up the work in June, 1894, she was spoken of as
"the youthful Secretary who throws her whole heart
and soul into the work."   She is the daughter of the
late Mr. Samuel Bamford, the Editor of the *Co-operative
News*, and gained from him not only an interest

Miss Bamford (now Mrs. Tomlinson).

in, and knowledge of, the Co-operative world, but also
wide democratic views and keen sympathy with her
fellows.   "I know," wrote one of the Lancashire
women, "she is the right person in the right place."
When she became Secretary of her Section there
were only 53 branches, but the number reached
100 in 1898, when a special fête was held in

Manchester, consisting of meetings, excursions, &c., to celebrate the occasion. The section now boasts 146 branches, some of which are the largest in the Guild, Darwen standing at the head with over 700 members.

Co-operative Societies are not so strong and numerous in the South as in the North, and Miss Spooner, who has been Secretary of the Southern Section since 1891, has not had the same amount of material and soil from which to develop her section, but she has been free to devote nearly the whole of her time to Co-operation. The work has been done remarkably well, and the members are not one whit less enthusiastic or educated Co-operators and citizens than their Northern sisters.

Miss Spooner came into the Guild as Secretary of the Hammersmith Branch, and as an advocate of an early Co-operative Orphanage scheme. She has since won for herself a unique place in the affection of the Southern branches by her practical helpfulness, her Irish geniality, and tireless energy. Her work has not been confined to the South, but she also helped, for a time, in the Midlands. She served on the Central Committee for four years, and is one of the women who sit on the governing bodies of the movement. (See page 102.)

This year the section has just held a demonstration at Woolwich, attended by 500 delegates and friends, to celebrate the formation of 100 branches. A conference took place in the afternoon, and in the evening Mr. Will Crooks, M.P. (for whose election the Woolwich Guildswomen worked so hard), presided. The other speakers were the old officials, Mrs.

MISS SPOONER.

D

Lawrenson and Miss Tournier, and the present General Secretary.

In connection with Sectional work, the two officials who have come next to Mrs. Tomlinson and Miss Spooner in length of service are Mrs. Adams, of Plymouth, who was Secretary of the Western Section from 1890–8, and Mrs. Carr, of Stockton-on-Tees, who was Secretary of the Northern Section from 1895–1900. They each served three years on the Central Committee, and each has been President of the Guild.

THE CENTRAL COMMITTEE.

We now come to that part of our own organisation which we call the "trunk" in the Guild Tree, namely, the Central Committee. It is formed of seven members, two elected by the North-Western Section, and one by each of the other sections, while the General Secretary is elected by all the branches throughout the Guild. There is much competition now to serve on the Central Committee, and great is the interest at Congress, when the elections are announced.

Some of the most animated debates at Congress have been on the question of the length of time members should sit on the Central Committee, some taking the view that a three years' limit is desirable, so as to leave room for others to come, others believing it a mistake to dispense with good and tried workers. At the present moment, the three years' limit* holds (except for the General Secretary).

---

* A three years' limit also exists in the sections and in most of the districts, except for the Sectional and District Secretaries.

The members forming the present Central Committee are Mrs. Mc.Blain (the President), who has been both a, Branch and a District Secretary; Mrs. Bury, Vice-President, who represents the Guild on the Co-operative Union Educational Committee; Mrs. Butterfield, a Yorkshire Poor-law Guardian; Mrs. Fidkin, who is a member of the Management Committee of her Society; Mrs. Green, who has served in a great variety of offices in the South, and is now a member of the Educational Committee of her Society; Mrs. Nightingale, who is also on the Educational Committee of her Society; and the General Secretary.

The Central Committee meet usually five times a year, and the work between the meetings is carried on by means of " Central Committee Circulars " through the post, owing to the expense of bringing seven persons together from all parts of England. Of recent years the meetings have been held at Leeds, where the Co-operative Society has kindly placed the Board Room at their disposal. In earlier years the meetings were in London, in Manchester, and frequently at Rugby, at the home of Miss Sharp (the former Editor of the " Woman's Corner ") during the time she was Vice-President of the Guild. Once there was a gathering, in which Sectional Secretaries were included, at the house of the present General Secretary in Kirkby Lonsdale, Westmorland, and the members saw the beautiful country in which the office of the Guild is situated.

The present Guild office could never be thought of

Mrs. Bury, *Vice-President*
(Darwen).

Mrs. Butterfield,
Treasurer (Keighley).

Mrs. Fidkin
(Bristol).

Mrs. McBlain, *President*
(Wallsend-on-Tyne).

Mrs. Green (Stratford)

Mrs. Nightingale
(Derby).

Miss Llewelyn Davies,
General Secretary.

PRESENT CENTRAL COMMITTEE.

F. Frith and Co., Ltd.] [Photographers.

KIRKBY LONSDALE.

apart from Miss Lilian Harris, who was living at Kirkby Lonsdale, when the office was removed there in 1889. She very soon became interested in the Guild, and in 1893 was appointed Cashier, and in 1901,* Assistant Secretary. Miss Harris attends to the whole Guild machinery, and is an "assistant" in everything. She has also written articles and papers on the Land Question, Free Trade, Old-Age Pensions, and other subjects.

The policy of the Guild and the direction of its work, lie in the hands of the Central Committee. Every autumn, what is termed a "Winter Circular" is issued to branches, in which suggestions for the year's work are made. It has become the custom to recommend in these circulars, in addition to perennial and varied Co-operative action, some special campaign in which all can take part.

Among the subjects which have been taken up the following may be mentioned :—Anti-credit Campaign, Investigation into the Hours of Co-operative Women Employés, Co-operative and Trade Union Alliance Campaign, Investigations into Conditions of Women Workers, Public Health, Co-operation and the Poor, Housing, Land, and Free Trade Campaigns.

Appropriate and specially written pamphlets and leaflets always accompany these campaigns. One of the duties of the Central Committee is to supply literature for the members, numerous original papers

* In this year, Miss Lucy Davenport (who also lived at Kirkby Lonsdale), held the post of Cashier, having previously been a helper in the office. Many articles in the "Woman's Corner" have come from Miss Davenport's pen, and it is to her we owe the popular pamphlet called "The Guild Office."

being published, dealing with all phases of Store and Co-operative life, with industrial, domestic, municipal and national questions, chiefly from the standpoint of women Co-operators. These papers are either sold for 1d. or are made into what are termed "popular" papers, and sent out on loan, to individuals, branches, or conferences.

In addition to what has been outlined above, the Central Committee has the spending of the Central Fund,* and it is expected that a large share of speaking work shall be done by each.

And last, but by no means least, it organises the Annual Congress of the Guild, the most important occurrence in the Guild's life each year.

After the Festival held in Manchester in 1892, when it was found that women could sustain such an event with credit, it was decided that the Guild should hold an annual meeting of its own, in the place of the meeting it had previously held at the time of the general Congress of the movement. It is an occasion our members look forward to through all the year, and those who go testify to the impression it makes upon them. A Southern member told the President of her branch that after she had been sent once (and paid for) by her branch, she was determined to go again. It took her two years to put by enough money, which she earned by doing a little washing or ironing on the quiet.

---

* It may be mentioned here, that all distinctly Guild work is done gratuitously, and that there are no paid officials on the Central Committee, nor in the Sections or Districts.

MISS LILIAN HARRIS,
Assistant Secretary.

KIRKBY LONSDALE VICARAGE
(showing Guild Office windows).

GUILD OFFICE.

A Northerner writes :—

"My first Congress was at Woolwich (1900). I never had such a good time in my life before ; the meetings were glorious, and the subjects we discussed were so helpful and practical that I felt we were within hailing distance of the great millennium. However, though I do not feel quite so sanguine, I am just as full of faith in the Guild to-day. My husband took his summer holiday when I went to Woolwich and stayed at home with the children and kept house for me. Since then we have generally had one of my sisters to stay or the children have gone to my mother for the week."

Our present Vice-President, Mrs. Bury, wrote as follows about the first annual meeting (Leicester, 1893) she attended :—

"It was a revelation. Each day my vision seemed to be widening, and my spirit felt that here was the very opportunity I had always been seeking, but never put into words. I had longings and aspirations and a vague idea of power within myself which had never had an opportunity of realisation. At the close of the meetings I felt as I imagine a war-horse must feel when he hears the beat of the drums. What I saw and heard at Leicester changed the whole course of my life for the next few years. My first impression was that the Guild was a great deal more powerful as a social lever than I had ever dreamt of. Altogether the business tone and the variety of subjects dealt with in such a practical way, combined with the good fellowship existing among the members, filled me with a wish to join hands in such a good cause. Since then my life in the Guild has been one long education."

Mrs. Bury began life early in her teens as a millworker in Lancashire. She is now a Poor-Law Guardian, and a foremost general of the Guild.

One of the most interesting of the annual Congresses was held at Doncaster in 1894.

In the presidential chair was Mrs. Ashworth, from Burnley, where from a very early age she had worked for twenty-one years, as a weaver in a cotton mill. She gave her address with deliberate utterance and a graceful dignity of deportment.

The order of proceedings was as follows:—Appointment of scrutineers of voting papers; reception of deputations (these included representatives from the Women's Trade Union Association, the Women's Suffrage Societies, and the late Frau Schwerin, of Berlin, our first foreign friend); then followed the discussion on the annual report, after which the delegates rose at 1 p.m. for luncheon, to meet again at 2-30. During the two days various subjects were discussed, including " Guild Organisation in Large Towns," by Mrs. Brown, of Burnley ; " Conditions of Women's Membership in Co-operative Societies," and " Women as Poor-Law Guardians," by Mrs. Abbott, of Tunbridge Wells.

After the sittings, came the sociable and lighter work of the Congress, including attendance at an organ recital in the fine old Parish Church, and a visit to the Free Library and Corn Exchange, ending with a procession of 400 women through the town to a reception in the Mansion House by the Mayor and Mayoress. During one evening the Central Committee held a Court, and presentations of visitors and officials—the Sectional Secretaries bearing their new banners—were made in amusing style, and an informal lesson on the organisation of the Guild given for the benefit of all. The third day was devoted to an excursion, as is invariably the rule at all our Congresses.

A CONGRESS EXCURSION.

CHAPTER III.

CO-OPERATIVE POLICY.

WE are continually being reminded by the appeals made to us to "purchase loyally" at the Store, that Co-operation might justly be called a woman's movement. Co-operators as consumers, and trade unionists as producers or workers, may be regarded as forming two halves of the same circle. And if a *man* be taken as the type of a worker, a *woman* would certainly represent a body of consumers or purchasers. It has been the aim of the Guild to arouse women to a sense of the "basket power" which they specially possessed.

Women's chief field of action is in Co-operative Stores, which are owned and managed by the members, who share the profits in the form of a dividend of, say, 2s. in the £ on purchases. The whole existence of a Store depends on the trade which the women bring to it. Their support is indispensable; therefore, "loyalty" is the first principle of the Guild. "Brass is gettin' spent at t'reet shop now," said a husband whose wife had just joined the Guild. "Hoo's noan goin' abeut lookin' for the chepest; hoo wants t'best noo."

E

" Aw know," a member was overheard to say, " ever so much more abeaut t' Store neow (after Guild mcetings). Aw feel as if t'were *my* shop."

A former Branch Secretary writes :—

"The many lessons on Co-operative work have given our members more ideas and better judgment in distinguishing between things better and things worse, and they are not the foolish prey to the exploiting huckster and hawker, or vendors of widows' tea, or offers of presents to sell shams. Simple working people have no greater pests than these to contend with. Agents go from door to door in the most overbearing manner, offering goods on the easy payment system."

The " divi.," by means of which remarkable savings are automatically made,* is undoubtedly the great magnet which attracts to Co-operation. It is only as members are educated in Co-operative ideals that they see other reasons for loyalty to the Store. Mrs. N., in speaking lately at a meeting, said she first joined for the sake of the dividend, but that now she "no longer hunts the ' divi.,'" owing to what she has learnt in the Guild. But neither the dividend nor Co-operative principles can always keep women loyal, especially when prices have been inflated in order to make unduly high dividends. A considerable strain is put on our members by the competition of outside shops. It is hard—often impossible—for the housewife with a large family and small wage to resist buying low-priced goods.

One of the outside attractions, to which even better-off Co-operative women sometimes fall a prey,

---

* The majority of Co-operators leave their dividend to accumulate in the Store, and as a result many are living in their own houses, or have laid by from £1 to £200.

is the plan of "giving away a present with a pound of
tea." As long ago as 1883, an excellent paper by
Mrs. Acland, entitled " Who pays for the tea-pots?"
appeared in the " Woman's Corner." She tells the
following story, which points the moral:—"An Irish-
man was found by a friend joining a long strip of
blanket on to the end of another piece of blanket.
'Oh, Pat,' says the friend, 'where did you get that
strip of blanket?' 'Why, sure,' says Pat, 'my blanket
was too short at the bottom entirely, and I just cut a
piece off the top to join on to it and make it a bit
longer.' "

But though "present-giving" and "bonus" teas have
their allurements for some (a few Societies catering for
this taste, though the C.W.S. no longer yields to it), they
have nothing like the attraction of the tea that brings
pensions on the death of husbands. This particular
mode of trading has become very prevalent of late
years. All Co-operators have not shown themselves
so stalwart as one of our members, who said at a
Guild meeting, "Ah bout ——'s tea for two weeks;
when ah looked at wor man he looked nowt like deeing,
so ah thowt ah'll gan ta th' Store for me tea, and th'
Guild for me night out." But it is impossible not to
sympathise with the need of providing against calamity.
It is only on the financial unsoundness of the pension
tea schemes, and the impossibility of constructing a
sound Co-operative one, that the whole practice has
been resisted by the Guild officials, with the support
of the majority of the delegates at the Guild Congress
last year.

After accepting *loyalty to the Store* as the foundation of Guild teaching, definite Co-operative principles
and practice have naturally and gradually been built
upon it. The Guild holds firmly to the belief of the
early pioneers, that industrial life must be based on
the ideals of justice, truth, and fellowship.

The Co-operative movement rests on the apparently
prosaic acts of buying and selling, but the prose may
almost be said to turn into romance when we see what
results may arise from this action. Few understand
at first how we may be helping or hindering to bring
about the reign of *justice* in the world, through
our shopping habits. The chance we have, is well
brought out by Mrs. Vaughan Nash in an early paper
she wrote for the Guild, called "Women's Duties as
Consumers." She says:—

"We know, of course, that the articles that are turned out
into the shops in such quantities do not, as they lie there, make
anyone's wealth, or health, or happiness. They are produced
with the idea that they will go further and be consumed in the
homes, and in order that the employer, who sets the work of
production going, may make a profit. But we hardly realise that
the consumer, through being the final object, *becomes the
controlling power*. Too much stress cannot be laid on the part
that consumption plays in controlling production and *use*, that is
to say, *in controlling work*. And seeing that the choice of articles
for consumption, or use, lies to a large extent in the hands of
the women who control the homes, it is evident that the place of
these women in the industrial system is a predominating one."

This idea soon came to dominate the Guild, and
a speech is seldom made by an official, without an
urgent appeal to the women not to buy "sweated"
goods, but encourage the best conditions of employment by giving their custom to the Co-operative

factories and workshops, where trade unionist conditions are observed, short hours are worked, and healthy accommodation provided.*

To stimulate such loyalty, small exhibitions have been held at Guild meetings, lists of Co-operative goods issued to branches, and innumerable expeditions have been made over Co-operative factories. Such keen Co-operators do Guild members become, that they have been indignant if the windows of their Stores were not dressed with Co-operative goods and advertisements, or if they were served with the goods of outside firms. At a Store in the southernmost part of England it was reported that if a Co-operative article were not stocked, twelve Guild women would go in turn and ask for it day after day, till they got it.

Naturally, that side of industrial conditions which comes most nearly home to us, is that which concerns our Co-operative Store employés, especially with regard to the hours worked. When the law of our country allows a young person in a shop to be worked 74 hours a week, and the hours for adult shop assistants are entirely unregulated, there is much need for enlightened views of employment. Co-operators were the first to institute the now accepted weekly half-

---

* Among Co-operative manufactures are Boots and Shoes, Soap, Jam, Biscuits, Flour, Woollen Materials, Ready-mades, Fustian, Bedsteads, Furniture, Printing, Cocoa, &c. In the 35 factories of the Co-operative Wholesale Society it is interesting to note that the hours in 19 are under 49 a week, in 5 are 48, and in 11 over 48, the longest hours being 55½ a week. The women and girls employed work very little legal overtime, and the newer buildings erected at Pelaw and Luton especially, are model factories:

holiday, and Co-operative hours and general conditions compare favourably with those of the outside world.*

In 1901, a hundred of our largest branches were asked if their members found any inconvenience in the early closing of Co-operative Stores, and the unanimous reply was that they found none at all.† And Guild women not only accept willingly the restricted shopping hours, but are amongst the first to propose and support reductions of hours at the quarterly meetings of Societies. The recent action of the Bury (Lancashire) Branch, which assisted in procuring a week's holiday, with pay, for their Store employés, is particularly gratifying. A more equitable distribution of holidays (without reduction of wages) is nearly as badly needed as a more equitable distribution of wealth. Factory workers, with their higher wages and greater independence, have taken the matter into their own hands, and the mills have to shut while the working population of Oldham, Burnley, and other Lancashire towns enjoy, for a week, the

---

* Many Co-operative Stores, especially in the Northern Section, have adopted the 48 hours week, and the half-holiday is a real one, beginning often at 12 noon. In 1895 the Guild carried out an investigation into the hours, wages, and conditions of women Store employés. The information which was given showed that, though there was room for improvement in some matters, the very long hours, the insufficient time allowed for meals, the practice of discharging without notice, and the custom of fines, were practically unknown in the Co-operative movement.

† Seventy-two branches (with a membership of 5,300 women) attached to 63 societies sent in replies. All declare that their members find no inconvenience in Co-operative hours, and 62 are of the opinion that late shopping is more of a habit than a necessity. This information was collected for a member of the Select Committee of the House of Lords on Lord Avebury's Bill for limiting shop hours. One of our London members, Mrs. Gasson, who was a witness at the Commission, explained that the Guild's desire for shorter hours was out of consideration for the health of the assistants and their need for leisure and education.

sea breezes of Blackpool, Morecambe, or the Isle of Man. It is time that those who sell the goods over the counter should be as well off, as regards conditions of employment, as those who make the goods in the mills.

Just as we try to secure *justice* in our conditions of employment throughout the Co-operative movement, so, in Store dealing, we try to uphold *truth.* The sale of pure unadulterated goods has been the Co-operative ideal from the time of the Rochdale Pioneers, and cash payments on the part of customers is their contribution to honest dealing.

In early Co-operative days, no goods were sold, unless paid for there and then, over the counter; but a large amount of credit dealing has gradually crept into the movement, and though it is hedged round with various restrictions, and is often only allowed for short periods, still, the practice is not viewed favourably by the Guild leaders nor by the majority of the branches, on account of its harmful effect on individuals and on Societies.*

In the discussions which have been held on this question, cases of distress were brought forward where

---

* An Anti-Credit campaign took place in the autumn of 1898, when papers on "Credit" were read at the five Sectional Conferences. At these the following resolution was passed:—"Every branch represented at this Conference, and connected with a Society where credit is allowed, pledges itself to urge its Society to adopt the ready-money system at the earliest possible opportunity." The next step was to appoint a Sectional Council member in each section to forward copies of the resolution to each branch, with a circular suggesting steps that might be taken, and asking for information as to whether credit was allowed. Replies came in from 116 out of about 260 branches. In the vast majority of cases they showed themselves most decidedly against credit, and resolutions were forwarded to Management Committees.

credit seemed a practical necessity. But it was also found that the richer customers were those who, as a rule, demanded credit, and for whose convenience, therefore, the poorer suffered; and it was felt that a better plan of meeting misfortune would be by the establishment of emergency funds, to tide over inevitable periods of distress.*

Co-operators saw from the beginning that the spirit of *fellowship*—summed up in the Co-operative motto, "Each for All, and All for Each," and applied in Co-operative practice—meant possibilities of knowledge and mental enjoyments, and the provision of a social life in which friendships and common aspirations should bind all the members together. Common funds, which all had helped to produce by associated action, have provided libraries and reading-rooms, bringing knowledge within the reach of all; and fine halls have been built, where the members could educate themselves in industrial and civic questions, where music could be performed, and pleasure sought in a society of friends. This educational policy, as it is called by Co-operators, not only brings advantages to individuals but is essential to the true progress of Co-operative Societies, for Societies cannot advance faster than their members. The higher the general standard of intelligence is in the rank and file of Co-operators, the more they are imbued with the

---

* This idea was started by Mrs. Boothman (Blackpool), who was President of the Guild in 1901, in a paper read at a North Lancashire District Conference in 1898. The subject was discussed at the five Sectional Conferences in the spring of 1899. Resolutions approving of emergency funds were passed both at these conferences and at the Annual Congress at Plymouth, 1899.

Co-operative faith, and the greater their civic aspirations, the better will it be for the Co-operative movement. This is the belief of the Guild; and while its chief work is to educate women and give them a wider life, it supports all attempts to extend this policy more widely throughout Societies.

The Guild has come into very close touch with—and, we may say, has considerably affected—the general educational action of the movement. Largely through the instrumentality of the Guild, a Special Committee was appointed at the Co-operative Congress in 1896, to inquire into the educational work of the movement. The General Secretary was a member of this Committee, and since that time the Guild has always been represented on the Central Educational Committee, and has thrown its weight not only into trying to improve direct Co-operative education, but to promote the wider learning and work of Co-operators as citizens.

The Guild considers that no Society is complete in its machinery for carrying out the ideals described in this chapter, unless it possesses what have been termed "the three wheels," i.e., a Management Committee, an Educational Committee, and a branch of the Guild. In some cases, branches have been the means of starting Educational Committees and Educational Funds, and are generally desirous of working in the closest harmony with them. For many years, branches and Educational Committees used to work aloof and independently, but. this is more and more seen to be a waste of energy, and "joint work" has become an accepted policy of the Guild. By this is meant working hand in hand with the various Committees, Associations, and Boards of the movement. Much progress has been made in this direction. Branches now .send deputations to Educational Committees to arrange "joint" winter programmes; round-table conferences of the three Committees are held; "joint" district conferences take place between Guild districts and District Associations of the Union, and, as will be seen in Chap. V., the organisations are not only working together, but individual women are more and more being elected as representatives and members, to sit side by side with men on the various Committees and Boards of the movement.

A further application of the fellowship ideal is seen in the propagandist work on which the Guild is actively bent. In the South, one of our members was employed, and with good results, in canvassing among members who had fallen away from Societies; while in other parts valuable help has been given in canvassing beforehand for meetings held to start Branch Stores, and in speaking at such meetings. Guild canvassers have naturally often come across the greatest ignorance. In one Northern village they were amused with an old woman who, finding the Store Manager would not exchange her checks for "a ha'porth of snuff," calmly threw them down the grating in front of her door. A short speech at a meeting from a woman, about the benefits she had herself derived from Co-operation and the dividend, would be more convincing to those who have the purchases to make, than strings of figures, showing the magnitude of Co-operative trade, rolled off by eloquent male speakers. But as yet the help of the Guild is not sought in this direction as much as it should be, if greater success is desired, for the enthusiasm of our members can generally be relied on.

The extension of Co-operation has usually taken place in the better-off artisan regions of town and country ; but a special effort, of which an account will be found in the following chapter, has been made of recent years, to bring Co-operation within reach of the poorest section of the community.

CHAPTER IV.

CO-OPERATIVE POLICY—continued.

CO-OPERATION IN POOR NEIGHBOURHOODS.

A PRAYER FOR THEM THAT BE IN POVERTY (*from Queen Elizabeth's Private Prayer Book, 1578*).—" Thou, O Lord, provideth enough for all men with Thy most liberal and bountiful hand, but whereas Thy gifts are, in respect of Thy goodness and free favour, made common to all men, we, through our naughtiness, niggardship, and distrust, do make them private and peculiar. Correct Thou the thing which our iniquity hath put out of order, and let Thy goodness supply that which our niggardliness hath plucked away."

"THERE is a vast population which practically we have not touched—they are as yet outside the pale of the movement. They ought to be in, and there is every reason why we should strive to bring them into the fold." These words, embodying a view that was a common-place on Co-operative platforms, were addressed to the Co-operative Congress, in 1899, by its President. They were taken up at the Congress by another speaker, who said:—" If we are to go down to the level of winning those who have not joined our movement, there was no agency which would do this better than the Women's Guild."

The Guild was glad to consider these remarks as in the nature of a challenge, and the result was that in a few months a paper, entitled, " Co-operation in Poor Neighbourhoods," was issued, and discussed at the five Sectional Conferences of the Guild.

The life in a poverty-stricken area was described in this paper, and it was pointed out that many of our Co-operative customs were not suited to the circumstances and habits of the poor, high dividends and high prices being the most effective barriers.

The suggestions made with a view to bringing Co-operation within the reach of the poorest, were as follows :—

(1) A People's Store, to supply wholesome food and other articles at cheap prices and in small quantities, to keep people out of debt by cash payment, and enable them to save automatically;

(2) A Coffee and Cooked Meat Shop;

(3) A Loan Department, taking security in the form of bondsmen, bills of sale, or personal property, so as to tide people over inevitable misfortunes, to lend without taking advantage of necessity, to ensure freedom from fraud, and to undermine the habit of weekly pawning;

(4) Club Rooms or Settlement, to be carried on by a special Propagandist Committee or resident workers, so as to attract from the public-house, to bring personal help, and form a centre of Co-operative activity in the district.

During our inquiries, we became aware of the work which was being done by the Sunderland and Plymouth Societies in Branch Stores situated in the poorest parts of those towns. The success of these branches was a great encouragement in advocating the further developments proposed in the Guild paper. A regular campaign now began on behalf of this scheme. A large number of conferences were held, more papers were written,* and letters and articles appeared in the *Co-operative News.*

An ardent response was at once made by many Guild members, but Co-operators as a whole, especially the men, did not take very kindly to the proposals. Varying reasons for inaction or opposition were given. For example: that the poor *had* become members under our present conditions and customs, which were all they should be; that if the poor did not avail themselves of the advantages of Co-operation, then they were not worth helping; that the scheme would be a purely charitable one, and could not possibly pay; that Co-operation was a business concern, and should, therefore, have nothing to do with it; that temperance was the only needed reform; or that education must precede all else. The Co-operative ground was covered with a hard crust, and a great deal of spade work had to be put into it, before it could take in the seed which the Guild was prepared to sow.

The point that raised the greatest opposition from both men and women was that of a loan department or reformed pawnshop. "The name 'pawnshop' has something revolting in it to most of us," said one woman. But at nearly all conferences, friends were found who welcomed the suggestion as an attempt to meet a real need. A supporter whose name will always be associated with this work—Mr. John Coley, then a

---

* "A Co-operative Colony," "Outline of a Scheme," "A Relief Column," "A Loan Department," "Cooked Meat Shops," "A People's Store."

member of the Sunderland Society's Board of Management—was first specially attracted to the scheme by the pawnshop proposal. Mr. Coley, formerly a railway employé, is Secretary of the Sunderland Charity Organisation Society. At a Northern Conference he said:—"In Sunderland they always inquired why members left the Store. Every week there were cases of withdrawal from out of work, because the money was absolutely required. They had tried over and over again to think out satisfactory schemes to meet this difficulty, but it passed the wit of man to do it fairly by means of relief. Now, he did believe in the pawnshop. Co-operators borrowed money on houses, why should it be less respectable to borrow money on the security of a watch? There is plenty of money in the movement, but we must take security. We should deal honestly with these people, and this would make all the difference." The proposal to reform the pawnshop has not at present had any practical result, but it was undoubtedly useful at the time, in attracting attention to the whole scheme.

At first the official bodies of the movement showed an unwillingness to take part in the work, as were so many of the rank and file. Vain efforts were made to induce both the United Board and the Propaganda Committee of the C.W.S. and Union, to form a Special Committee jointly with the Guild. So the Guild was forced to work alone, but the United Board agreed to grant a sum not exceeding £50, in order that the Guild might undertake an inquiry for which it should alone be responsible. The object of the inquiry

was (1) to investigate the present customs of the
Co-operative movement in their bearing on the poorer
classes of society, and (2) to show what Co-operation
might do towards solving the problem of poverty in
large towns. The report of this inquiry was published
in 1902.

The work, broadly speaking, fell into two divisions:
(1) An investigation into the rules and customs as
regards admission, share capital, dividends, penny
banks, clubs; into prices; and into the frozen meat and
coal trade; (2) in addition, certain towns—Sheffield,
Bury, York, Newcastle, Sunderland, Plymouth, and
Bristol—were selected, and the poorest area in each per-
sonally explored. The characteristic money and trading
customs were observed in these localities, the people
were visited in their homes, local town officials were
interviewed, and conferences between the Management,
Educational, and Guild Committees were held with
the Guild investigators, who reported on their work
and suggested action which the local Societies might
take.

This inquiry formed the basis for more specialised
suggestions. In these, every reform of a financial
character was taken from the practice of some Society,
and was therefore practicable; while the business and
social work which could be carried on in a group
of Co-operative buildings, was further enlarged on.

The Co-operative Congress, in 1902, recommended
Societies to discuss the report of the inquiry at District
Conferences, and for this purpose another paper, entitled,
"The Open Door," was published, which has been sold

in thousands, and discussed throughout the movement. This title has come to represent the policy of doing away with obstacles to the entry of the poor into the movement. The Guild believes in all Societies taking down such barriers as entrance fees and high dividends.

It is no justification of entrance fees to say that many poor people have paid them in the past, in order to benefit by Co-operation. When bread was dear, people paid the price as far as they could, but reduction in price means that more bread is bought. And to abolish the entrance fee, converting the shilling or two-shilling fee into a deposit to share capital, means that more people will become Co-operators.

So, again, reduced dividends and prices will mean increased custom and customers. Women understand, as few men do, that high prices are an insurmountable barrier to loyalty or membership. When a man earns, say, 18s. a week, retains two or three shillings as pocket money, and there is a family of six children to be kept, his wife is obliged to think of quantity before quality, however uneconomical it may be. When dinners have to be made of "onions fried in dripping and boiled potatoes, or the scraps of bacon and a ha'porth of liver fried together for gravy to eat with potatoes," how can the family buy at the Store, if the articles sold there are twopence or one penny dearer, owing to the handsome dividend of three shillings or more, that is demanded as a convenient form of saving, by the better-off Co-operators? In desiring low prices, the Guild realises it must

F

accept a moderate dividend, say, of from 1s. 6d. to
2s. 6d., according to the special local conditions.*

The Guild is justly proud that one of its members
should have made an outspoken protest at a quarterly
meeting against an additional penny being added to
the dividend. Mrs. Bury, at Darwen, in 1901, said
she took exception to the policy of adding the profit
to dividend, instead of using it in the reduction of
prices. She claimed to be an enthusiastic Co-operator,
and said that in trying to make Co-operators, she was
frequently met with the objection that prices were too
high. If Committees would screw their courage to
the sticking point and reduce high dividends as
opportunity arises, there could be no doubt they would
find many warm supporters.

While the Guild was advocating the policy of the
"open door" as applicable to all Societies and more
consistent with the spirit of fellowship, a group of
Co-operative buildings, on the lines suggested by the
Guild, was rising in Sunderland. The Sunderland
Society had already been experimenting by planting
branches in some of the most congested regions of
the town. The grocer's shop in the new block was to
take the place of a small rented shop, where a mongoose
had been kept on the premises to prevent the leakage
caused by rats.

---

* The following resolution was passed at the Guild Congress in 1897 :—
"That the Women's Co-operative Guild is of opinion that Co-operators should
discourage the payment of a rate of dividend higher than is consistent with
a just regard to reasonable charges for goods, liberal treatment of employés,
efficient safeguarding of the stability of the Society, and ample provision for
the intellectual and social needs of its members."

It was a red-letter day for Sunderland and the Co-operative movement when the corner premises of the Branch Store in Coronation Street were opened on October 8th, 1902. The name "Coronation Street" has become a household word in the movement, so great and widespread has the interest of Co-operators become in the Sunderland experiment. Coronation Stree is the narrow shopping thoroughfare, full of chandlers' and butchers' shops,

GROCERY STORE, CORONATION STREET SUNDERLAND.

public-houses, chip saloons, and "London wardrobes," for the inhabitants of the numberless dark lanes which open out of it. The Branch Store is in the very heart of the most overcrowded part of Sunderland, between Spring Garden Lane and Golden Alley, a region which has the highest record of death, disease, and crime. Here the Sunderland Co-operators have chosen to bring Co-operation, coming with the idea, not that "nothing is too bad for the poor," as a poor woman said, but that nothing is too *good* for the poor.

The bright new Store buildings consist of a grocer's shop (where Mr. Hart, the Manager, presides, with four assistants), a butcher's shop, flour store, a hall

---

SUNDERLAND
Equitable Industrial Society,
Limited.

PURE MILK SUPPLY.

THE

Co-operative Store

IN

CORONATION STREET

WILL SELL

MILK

Every afternoon from 3 to 5 o'clock in pennyworths and half-pennyworths,

Checks given.

The best food for Children is MILK.

Cheap Tinned Milk contains very little nourishment.

Come and buy
    Pure Co-operative Milk,
    4d. per quart.

---

and small rooms for two resident workers. There are no shop windows in the street to compare with the Co-operative ones. Plate glass and electric light show off the pile of Co-operative loaves at 1d. and 2½d., or an ingeniously arranged show of C.W.S. 1d. goods:— pots of jam and marmalade, tins of tea and syrup, bottles of hair and castor oil, &c. Sometimes the cheapest drapery fills one of the windows, and a great bill announces a special sale in the hall; while various notices are pasted up announcing, it may be, the sale of milk at 4d. a quart, or the variety of entertainments and meetings going on in the hall upstairs.

BUTCHER'S SHOP AND SETTLEMENT, CORONATION STREET, SUNDERLAND.

The butcher's corner window is equally attractive with its steaming hot boiled joints of pork at 1s., or shanks at 5d.; hot pease pudding, with gravy, ½d. and 1d.; tripe, 4d. and 5d.; brawn, 5d. The sale of hot soup, at ½d. and 1d., was found so popular and such a financial success, that it was introduced with equally good results into a neighbouring east-end Branch Store.

Turning round the corner into Walton Place there is a door, probably with children on the step, leading up a narrow staircase to the little hall, gay with white and green paint, pictures, electric light, and bright red fustian curtains from the Hebden Bridge Co-operative Society.   Opposite the hall, over the butcher's shop, is the sunny kitchen of the "Store

SUNDERLAND SETTLEMENT.
Corner showing Leadless-Glaze
Crockery.

ladies," which has to serve as office, sitting-room, kitchen, and be used for tea parties, for boiling kettles to make the ½d. cups of tea for the hall concerts, and for any other purpose that is wanted. Much thought was given to the furnishing of the rooms, so as to make them as simple, cheer-ful, and Co-operative as possible. Inside the kitchen, with its pale, pink-washed walls and white paint, the shelves gay with "open rose" leadless-glaze crockery, the big windows free from any sort of blinds, and hung with washable pink tulip-patterned curtains, anyone might forget the outside surroundings, were it not for the rain of big black smuts, the loud voices of the children, the street fights, the "Hallelujah Chorus" on an organ, the trumpet of a little man exchanging rags and bones for whiting and candy, or the cries of the neighbouring butcher to the unresponding passers-by.

The tiny scullery, in which a bath has been put, with a lid to form a table, is thought "very canny." Two of the five doors of the small kitchen open into the diminutive bedrooms looking into Coronation Street, where the return home of the people when the public-houses close, the terrible drunken rows, and the rumbling of the Corporation carts over the cobbles in the middle of the night, are sounds to which the occupants have to become accustomed.

The Society welcomed every suggestion to make the whole place as attractive as possible, and in front of the seven upstairs windows are window boxes filled, according to the time of year, with golden (though smutty) crocuses and daffodils, or geraniums, forming a bright coloured wreath round the building.

For the first three months the organisation of the work at the Settlement was entrusted by the Society to the General Secretary of the Guild, and during this time she was helped by Miss Spooner, Miss Partridge, Mrs. Abbott, and Miss Mayo. At the end of that period Miss Partridge was appointed as the permanent worker. She had help from various Guild members in succession (and for three months from Miss E. T. Orme), till the beginning of this year, when Miss Rushworth, of Halifax, who was one of the Guild's District Secretaries, was appointed as a second resident.

On the right, as you enter the grocery shop is

a desk, behind which the "Store ladies" are to be found every day at certain times, making friends with the people, and doing business at the same time. Here members are made,* deposits are taken towards the 1s. entrance fee and towards share capital, and pennies are put on club books. The Store forms an admirable ground for propagandist work of all kinds, and the desk is often covered with small cards and notices of meetings.

But the biggest piece of work at the desk is the Penny Bank, the news of which spread like wild-fire among the children as soon as it started.† The children have been used to the idea of small savings through " sweet clubs " and " boxes " (kept by widows generally, into which the children pay one penny per week, and of which fourpence in the 4s. 4d. is retained as payment at the end of the year). But most of the pence used to go in " bullets," or chips, or cigarettes. The desk has become a centre of life and interest to the children of the neighbourhood, to whom a word of special praise must be given. They become real friends, full of fun, very affectionate, and never rude, though at times they have made us much too conscious of their

---

* The new members made have been as follows:—First three months, 186 fully paid up entrance fees; twelve months, January 8th, 1903, to January 8th, 1904, 127 fully paid up entrance fees; 40 still paying by instalments; total, 303. More than 30 per cent of the new members have paid or are paying their entrance fees by instalments. In the old Coronation Street shop only 178 members were made in four years.

† The numbers joining the Penny Bank have been as follows:—First three months, 674; 12 months, January 8th, 1903, to January 8th, 1904, 942—1,616; withdrawn, 365; total in Penny Bank, January 8th, 1904, 1,251. The following figures show in what small amounts savings are in such a neighbourhood. They refer to the period from October 8th, 1903, to September 3rd, 1904:—38 had paid in over £1, 163 over 5s., 702 between 1s. and 5s., 501 less than 1s., 145 once only.

presence at the front door. But it is disarming when a "settler" goes down to open the door, thinking there is someone there on business, to find a little girl whose only remarks are, " Miss ——, I've come to seek ye ; I want to be by yer side;" or to find two little girls, with shawls over their heads, have come to say that both their dolls were in bed "with lots of clo' on, and dreaming about a tea party." Many are the confidences made at the desk, to which the children feel they have a right to come. A little bare-footed fellow will dash in with a counterpane over his shoulder, just to mention he'd " been to the pop ; " another will bring a rat in a cage, caught during the night; or on Saturday a small girl tells that she is "going to be weshed arl over, head an arl." A child of 16, who came one day to deposit, was asked how it was she was so small, and in a calm, old-fashioned manner replied, " I've been kep' down by minding babies." " How many? " " Me mother's had 13, and I've minded eight."

There is hardly a day in the autumn and winter when the hall upstairs is not used for some purpose or other. One of the best times to see it is on Tuesday nights, when the concert party, which has become a regular institution in the neighbourhood, takes place. Beginning with an audience of 15, the hall, which will hold about 100, is now crowded out every week. Co-operative and other friends provide entertainments and Co-operative talks, and the local children are always delighted to recite and sing.

A variety of meetings for women, young women, boys, and children have gone on since the opening, and a library is also now in use. A Branch of the Guild has been formed, of which Miss Rushworth is Secretary. A feature of the early months, which has since been dropped, was the Sunday evening discussions for men.

It is not possible, for various reasons, to give a descriptive personal account of the people of the neighbourhood. The usual customs of pawning, drinking, and fighting prevail, and the overcrowding is occasionally terrible ; but these habits do not mean that there is not much that is good and attractive in

the characters of the men and women. Connection with the Store acts as an "open sesame" to their homes. At a house visited in a wretched street, a group of women were collected in a semi-underground room. When Mrs. A. was asked for, no one spoke or

NEXT DOOR TO THE SETTLEMENT.

came forward ; but when a young woman peered from behind the screen and remarked "It's t'Store," Mrs. A. emerged from the gloom, and gratefully accepted the card of invitation to the Tuesday party.

Visits are made to those who are on the way to becoming members, and pence are collected towards the shilling entrance fee. Besides these promiscuous

calls, special streets are visited systematically. This
enables friendships to grow, and impressions to be
made. The men of the neighbourhood belong largely
to the class of labourers connected with the shipyards,
and many of the women are hawkers of fish, &c. The
girls are employed in "baccy" and brewery works, or
in little "places," and the children sell papers, oranges,
winkles, or whatever turns up handily, and do errands
for neighbours for pennies.

A FAMILY IN WALTON PLACE.

At special seasons great efforts are made to paper
and clean the houses, and to bring the children out
in fresh clothes. Then raps may be heard at the
door of the Settlement, and an elder sister will appear
with a baby in a new frock and clean pinafore, tied up
with pink ribbons, and say, "Please Miss ——, baby's
come to have her photo taken," as Miss —— is known
to take snap-shots. Space will not permit a description

of all the varied life that the Store has brought, but mention should especially be made of days in the country, expeditions over the central premises, with the 3d. teas in the Co-operative café, the May-day procession, and the great Christmas entertainment of the Penny Bankers.

The gloomy forebodings of those who prophesied financial failure, have proved entirely groundless, and it is hardly too much to say that if conducted on proper lines—low dividend, low prices, smart shops, cooked food, and propagandist work—Stores in such neighbourhoods could not fail to succeed. The Sunderland Society has now bought the house adjoining the Store, as the premises are too small, and they desire to extend the business to coal (which is bought in pennyworths by the people) and oil. The tables of figures at the close of this chapter will show how well, in spite of bad times, the "poor" Store compares with its richer sister branches.

To sum up what so far seems to have been proved by the noble pioneer work done by the Sunderland Co-operators, we may say that—(1) it is possible to win the trade of the poorest; (2) that such trade is a financial gain to the whole Society; (3) that the Store is a sure means for gaining the confidence and friendship of the people, establishing a relationship built on self-help and unspoilt by the demoralising effects of charity; and (4) that the Store might become a foundation and centre for constructive social work in parts where it is most needed. At present it is only a beginning which has been made, and what is being done is on quite a

Announcements of "Record" Sales, left late on Saturday Nights in the Settlement Letter Box.

small scale. But the essential point is that the work rests on a solid basis—that of the primary, necessary acts of life. To start by getting these on to satisfactory, self-respecting lines gives a solidity to whatever educational work is afterwards built upon them. Therefore, Co-operators, if they have the *will*, possess to an almost unlimited degree, the power to raise the whole standard of individual and social life in poor areas.

Those who are concerned with the problem of poverty are beset with anxious and baffling problems. It is easy to learn by experience that promiscuous giving only produces evils, but it is not easy to be reconciled to any suppression of compassionate instincts, nor easy to rest in the negative, estranging policy of trying to separate the "sheep" from the "goats."* Is it possible that those who seek to help the poor are baffled because they are not ready for a remedy, involving deeper sacrifices than have yet been made, a change in life's conditions, when "the odious words 'rich' and 'poor' will be wiped out of our

* These ideas have been suggested by an interesting passage on the subject of "Charitable Effort," in a book called "Democracy and Social Ethics," by Miss Jane Addams, the Warden of a great Social Settlement in Chicago, U.S.A. She writes:—

"The Hebrew Prophet made three requirements from those who would join the great forward-moving procession led by Jehovah. 'To love mercy' and at the same time 'to do justly' is the difficult task; to fulfil the first requirement alone is to fall into the error of indiscriminate giving with all its disastrous results; to fulfil the second solely is to obtain the stern policy of withholding, and it results in such a dreary lack of sympathy and understanding that the establishment of justice is impossible. It may be that the combination of the two can never be attained, save as we fulfil still the third requirement—'to walk humbly with God,' which may mean to walk for many dreary miles beside the lowliest of His creatures, not even in that peace of mind which the company of the humble is popularly supposed to afford, but rather with the pangs and throes to which the poor human understanding is subjected whenever it attempts to comprehend the meaning of life."

vocabulary?" Perhaps it is only by embracing and acting on such a belief that difficulties will disappear, and brotherly love be able to become simple, and free, and universal.

And to bring about this transformation individual action alone will not suffice. Large municipal and national reforms are necessary before stricken areas can be freed from all that trades on ignorance, poverty, and misfortune.

TRADE FIGURES.

CORONATION STREET BRANCH STORE
(SUNDERLAND SOCIETY).
GROCERY DEPARTMENT.

HALF YEAR ENDING	Sales—Coronation Street.	Profit per £ of Sales.		Expenses per £ of Sales.		Leakage per £.		Debts Owing.	
		Coronation Street.	Average of Grocery Branches.	Coronation Street.	Average of Grocery Branches.	Coronation Street.	Average of Grocery Branches.	Coronation Street.	Other Grocery Branches.
	£	s. d.	s. d.	s. d.	s. d.	s. d.	s. d.		£ s. d.
January, 1903..	2547	2 1¾	2 2½	1 5¼	1 3¾	..	0 3¾	..	..
July, 1903	3172	2 1¼	2 3¾	1 4¾	1 3½	0 1¾	0 4½	..	51 10 0
January, 1904..	2967	2 2¼	2 1¼	1 7¼	1 4½	0 0¼	0 3¾	..	27 8 0
	8686	..	..	..	..	..	..	..	..

The first half year only includes four months in the new buildings, which were opened on October 8th, 1902. In the first half year, out of 24 Grocery Branches, six made the same or less profit, seven had the same or higher expenses, 24 had smaller sales than Coronation Street. In the second half year, five made the same or less profit, eight had the same or higher expenses, and seven had smaller sales than Coronation Street. In the third half year, 16 out of 25 Grocery Branches made less profit, five had the same or higher expenses, and nine had smaller sales.

BUTCHERY DEPARTMENT.

HALF YEAR ENDING	Sales—Coronation Street.	Profit per £ of Sales.		Expenses per £ of Sales.		Debts Owing.	
		Coronation Street.	Average of Butchery Depts.	Coronation Street.	Average of Butchery Branches.	Coronation Street.	Other Butchery Branches.
	£	s. d.	s. d.	s. d.	s. d.	£ s. d.	£ s. d.
January, 1903	1549	2 6½	1 8¾	1 5½	2 2¼	1 18 0	50 8 0
July, 1903	2070	1 5	0 9	1 4	1 11¾	0 11 0	72 19 0
January, 1904	1724	2 4¼	1 6½	1 9	2 4	1 11 0	199 17 0
	5343	..	..	..	..	..	..

In the first half year the Butchery Department was only open for four months. Out of 17 Butchery Branches, Coronation Street has had the largest sales and made the highest profits per £ since it was opened. No branch had lower expenses per £ the first half year, and only two in the second half year and one in the third had lower expenses.

*　*　*　*　*　*　*　*

The Bristol Society opened a small branch in the poorest locality of the town in 1901. The trade done for the first week was £15, this year it is about £60. Hull and Stockton Societies are also experimenting, and at Sheffield the Brightside and Carbrook Society have a scheme in contemplation.

G

CHAPTER V.

EQUALITY OF OPPORTUNITY.

TO the credit of the Co-operative movement it may be said that, as a whole, it has opened its doors to women on the same terms as men. The rules of the majority of Societies admit to membership any adult man or woman, and this opportunity is largely taken advantage of by different members in a family. "In our house," writes a Guild Secretary, "my husband is a member, I am one, and my two sons and one daughter, and my sister who lives with me, are all members." But some Societies have unfortunately departed from this rule of "open membership," and a variety of rules have been substituted which have largely the effect of shutting out the women. For example, in some Societies only one in a family is allowed to be a member; in others, either a husband *or* wife, and grown-up children may be members; or joint membership between husband and wife is alone allowed; while in a few Societies there are customs which definitely exclude a wife, or demand her husband's permission before admitting her as a member. Such customs seem to remove us very far from the rules of an old Society, where a husband could only become a member with his wife's consent.

In some cases we find husbands, who are not themselves interested in Co-operation, recognising that their wives are the real Co-operators, and willing to arrange an exchange of membership. A Guild member, whose husband was the Store member, urged him so effectually that he attended a quarterly meeting for the first time in twenty years. He found it "little in his line," and told his wife—"t' sooner yo gets my name takken off and yer own putten on as t' member, t' better it'll be." But Guild members are very loth to deprive their husbands of rights, however much they may desire to exercise their own.

Apart from other reasons, it is often of the greatest importance to women to be members, so as to be able to accumulate a little money in the Store in their own names. Even in the days when there was no Women's Property Act it was a benefit to women. Mr. Holyoake tells us that in cases where a woman had a drunken husband who came to claim his wife's Store money, Storekeepers would refuse to give it him, although knowing he was legally entitled to it.

It seems that the ground of the departure from the principle of equality has probably been due, not to any feeling of hostility to women, but to the desire to limit the amount of share capital in Societies. But this cannot be accepted as an argument by the Guild. If Societies are not strong or enterprising enough to deal with any amount of capital the members wish to invest, there are various ways of meeting the situation without practically excluding married women. We are bound to admit that the unwillingness to restore "open membership" seems now to be based to some extent on jealousy, and a desire to close the Co-operative

doors to women because of the positions they might
win in the movement.   Women are claiming their
rights because the Guild has taught them their duties.
Without equal opportunities, the knowledge and enthusiasm with which they desire to serve their Societies
has quite insufficient outlet.

Therefore, it is not surprising that for many years
the Guild has been contending for "open membership"
in all Societies, and urging branches to take action
to obtain the necessary alteration of rule.   Success has
been met with in some cases, in others the battle has
been temporarily lost, and in many the field has still
to be taken.   "Open membership" exists in most of
the largest and most flourishing Societies—for example,
in Leeds, Bolton, Plymouth, Woolwich, and Sunderland.
In some Societies the women members outnumber
the men, and in the whole movement there are
hundreds of thousands of women holding shares in
their own names.

Where the membership of a Society has been
"open," great is the change which the Guild has
effected as regards the attendance of women at quarterly
meetings of Societies.   "Are those widows or are they
wanters?" was a question unwittingly addressed to
the husband of an adventurous Scotch woman, who
made bold one evening to attend a quarterly meeting.
So unusual a sight caused the women to be looked
on as strange beings with an ulterior motive.   But
the Guild has brought about a very different state
of things.   "Before our branch was started," wrote
a Guild Secretary, "there was scarcely a woman

to be seen at our quarterly meeting, and it was quite a talk if one should happen to drop in. Now they take it quite as a matter of course." Once admitted, through membership, to quarterly meetings, all else in the way of election to Committees, Boards, meetings, &c., becomes possible, although prejudice and certain restrictive customs place great obstacles in women's paths.

It has not been the policy of the Guild to seek special representation for itself as a body, but to prepare women, and open up chances for them, so that they may take their places on a footing of equality beside the men throughout the movement.

The table at the end of this chapter will show how far we have advanced in representation in the movement. Although progress is being made, it will be seen that much still remains to be done. The number of women on Management Committees is much smaller than on Educational Committees, for which fact there are various reasons—the principal one being the amount of time demanded from members of Management Committees. "But I will venture to say," writes a woman who has had experience on the Board of a large Society, "that no Store, however good, can be properly managed *without* a woman on its Management Committee, because there are things a man (even the best man) does not see, or if he does see he only sees his own side of. He will modify and improve his views when the other side is shown to him—at least that is my experience." A point which women often seize on more quickly than men is the need for sanitary reforms; while the large number of women Co-operative employés is a strong argument in favour of women being members of the Committees which employ them. Both on Management and Educational Committees the women have often made themselves much valued colleagues. Twice, in different parts of the country, the same observation was made by two men about two of our Guild members—" She's the best man on the Committee."*

It is also most desirable that women should sit on the governing Boards of the Co-operative Union, which is a Federation of Co-operative Societies, directing the general policy of the movement, and carrying out its educational and propagandist work. The first woman to gain a seat on the Southern Sectional Board was Mrs. Lawrenson, who was elected in 1893. Then followed Miss Webb, who became its first woman Chairman, and now Miss Spooner and Mrs. Abbott are both members.

Miss Reddish and Mrs. Bury have tried several times for a seat on the North-Western Sectional Board, but though coming very near neither has yet succeeded.

POSITION OF GUILD WOMEN IN THE MOVEMENT,
1904.

Chairman of United Board of Co-operative Union: Miss Spooner
Central Co-operative Board (Southern Section): Miss Spooner
and Mrs. Abbott.

---

*One of our branch Presidents in the South has been for some years Secretary of her Society, and it is not too much to say that it is due to her untiring work that the Society has been gradually raised to its present satisfactory condition.

Educational Committee, Co-operative Union : Mrs. Bury (representing the Women's Co-operative Guild); Mrs. Abbott (Southern Sectional Board).

Educational Committees Association : Eleven Guild Members.

South Metropolitan District Association : Mrs. Gasson (Secretary).

Convalescent Scheme Committees : Three Guild Members.

Number of Wcmen on Management Committees : 30 in 20 Societies.

Number of Women on Educational Committees : 238 in 108 Societies.

C.W.S. Quarterly and Divisional Meetings : 60 to 70 woman appointed as Delegates from 26 Societies.

Co-operative Congress : 16 women as Delegates from 14 Societies.

Editors of "Wheatsheaf" Pages and "Records": Five women, in five Societies.

CHAPTER VI.

THE CONVALESCENT FUND.

A NATURAL desire to commemorate in some way the life and work of the late Mrs. Benjamin Jones led, in 1895, to the formation of the "Mrs. Jones Guild Convalescent Fund." It had first been suggested that the memorial should take the form of a cot in a children's hospital, but this idea was abandoned, and at the London Congress, in 1895, the delegates voted that the money subscribed should be used for sending away Guild members who were in need of change and rest. It was decided that the £200 which had been raised, partly by branch and individual subscriptions, and partly by the gift of £60 from an anonymous donor, should be invested with the Co-operative Union at 4 per cent; also, that the fund should be kept permanently open, and be administered by a Sub-Committee of representatives appointed by the Sectional Councils, the General Secretary being an *ex officio* member.

In 1896 the Guild had the great good fortune to secure Mrs. Abbott (of Tunbridge Wells) as its Secretary. Since that time the interest taken in the fund, the constant increase in subscriptions, and the number of applicants helped in a wise and satisfactory manner, has been owing chiefly to the skill and zeal of her management.   Whatever work Mrs. Abbott's public spirit leads her to take up—whether the duties of a Store Secretary, or of a member of a Co-operative

MRS. ABBOTT.

or Technical Educational Committee—her practical ability and devotion make her an expert.

Mrs. Abbott describes the varying methods of help as follows, from which it will be seen that elasticity and adaptability to special cases, combined with great economy, are characteristic of the rules and management of the fund, and make it of special value to women :—

(1) Grant of £1, to provide own board and lodgings, and reasonable fares, generally limited to 10s., as a good change of air can always be found within a radius of 60 miles. This is the favourite form of help, as so many have relatives or friends who are glad to receive them.

(2) Convalescent homes and fares, recommended when the illness has been serious, and some attendance from doctor or nurses or special diet is still required.

(3) Co-operative lodgings and fares. This means that the Secretary of the fund keeps a list of Guild members living in healthy, pleasant places, who are willing to receive our convalescents for a payment from the fund of 10s. or 12s. a week.

(4) Fares only, for those who can get a holiday with friends or in some other way, but cannot find the ready money for the railway ticket.

(5) Expenses of help at home, incurred owing to absence of convalescent. This in the case of a widow with little children, or any woman who is the sole support of her household, is sometimes added to one of the other forms of help.

For the first years, all subscriptions were added to capital, and only interest was used. But Mrs. Abbott, holding the view that it is better for each generation to bear its own burden, and that it is best for expenditure to be in the hands of those who supply the money, proposed in 1897 that branches should be allowed to subscribe their money *for present use*, instead of as donations to capital. Thus a much larger yearly income was obtained, and many more applicants could be helped.

During the first year of the fund's existence there were twenty-six applicants, but the interest on the capital—£8—was only enough to help seven. Of these, three were sent to convalescent homes, two to Co-operative lodgings, and two had their fares paid to enable them to stay with friends. This year (1904) the number helped and the contributions received have exceeded those of any other year. The income amounted to £125. 11s. 9½d., and seventy-eight convalescents were sent away. The capital now amounts to £325, yielding £13 in interest. During the last two years, 183 branches and three Societies have contributed to the fund. The total number of cases helped since June, 1896, is 315.

Contributions to the fund are entirely voluntary, and the ideal aimed at is that each member of the Guild should contribute 1d. annually, so that all helping equally, it should be felt to be a matter of *insurance* and not charity, when aid from the fund is needed.

NOTE.—During the last few years, the establishment of Convalescent Homes has occupied the attention of the movement. To the three already in existence in England and Scotland, three others will shortly be added. Guild women are taking a great interest in this new move. But there is a strong feeling among many in favour of *Funds* as against *Homes*. The Southern Section of the Union has decided in favour of a Fund, and the matter is under discussion in the South-Western Section.

CHAPTER VII.

THE "WOMAN'S CORNER" OF THE
CO-OPERATIVE NEWS.

IT has been mentioned in Chapter I. that a new feature was introduced into the *Co-operative News* on January 1st, 1883. A page called the "Woman's Corner" was set aside specially for women, and the editing of it was entrusted to Mrs. Arthur Acland. Since that time the "Woman's Corner," though never

MRS. ACLAND.

controlled by the Guild, has always been practically accepted by both Editors and Guild members as the organ of the Guild, and been of signal service to it. Mrs. Acland says she "got leave for a 'Woman's Corner' in the *News* with very great difficulty." There was considerable opposition to such an intrusion, and had it not been for the support of the late Editor, Mr. Samuel Bamford, it is quite possible the "Corner" might never have seen the light.

In those days women's domestic needs were not catered for as they are now in endless penny papers and "pages for the home," nor by the technical classes of local authorities. " The demand for clothes, patterns, the anxious call for cooking recipes (three or four letters a day would come asking for them), and details of household advice—all bombarded one weekly," says Mrs. Acland. But other thoughts were also stirring in the women's minds, and there were those ready to take advantage of any opening for wider life, as is shown by occasional letters, and by the immediate proposal to start the Guild.

How well Mrs. Acland tried to meet all tastes is seen in the excellent articles which appeared week by week. She herself contributed papers on "Health," "Economical Cookery," "Children's Books." "Gifts of Our Century (Trains, Gas, Fire Brigade, &c.)," by Sarah Brook, formed another series; M. E. Palgrave contributed several articles on "Great Painters;" Co-operative and Guild papers and reports had also, of course, a place; while two valuable series of papers came out the first year, called "Factory Acts and Women's Work," by R. M. Fry, and "Legal Protection for Young Girls," by Miss Sharp, whose name then first appears in connection with Co-operation. Amongst the earliest contributors who were most faithful in writing for the "Corner" were Miss E. C. Wilson and Miss M. S. Talbot.

In June, 1884, Miss Sharp became Assistant Editor to Mrs. Acland, whose ill-health compelled her for nearly a year previously to leave the editorial work almost entirely in Miss Sharp's competent hands. But Mrs. Acland's interest in and enthusiasm for the "Corner" and Guild never failed, and, although at last forced to relinquish the editorship, she devised a special post and work for herself in connection with "Prize Essays." Every kind of subject was ingeniously thought of and dealt with for many years, and the papers of the competitors carefully read and classed. One of our Guild members, Mrs. Moxon, of Sheffield, carried off thirty-one prizes. The certificate card was designed by Miss Alice Thompson, a friend of the artists Wm. Morris and F. Shields.

MISS SHARP.

During these years the Guild was growing, and asking room for all sorts of papers, reports of conferences, branch reports, and Miss Mayo's tours, while the space (two pages) in the "Corner" remained the same. How best to deal with Guild matter has exercised, and still exercises, the wit of both Editor and Guild officials. "Notes from the Central Committee," by Miss Webb, began to appear in 1893. These formed a useful link between the branches and the centre, and continued for some years, and then changed into "Office Letters." But the problem of the branch reports, as they became more and more numerous, while the Secretaries became no more willing to have them curtailed, has not been solved to this day. Various different plans have been tried—district compilers, sectional summaries, systematised half-yearly reports—and it has been proposed that the Guild should start a separate paper of its own. But the value of having the "Woman's Corner" incorporated with the *News*, and so keeping the Guild

in touch with the whole movement and in evidence before it, has been too great to be dispensed with.

On August 15th, 1896, appeared an article entitled "Good-bye," signed by Miss Sharp, in which she explains that as her home at Rugby was breaking up, and other work might claim her, she feels it best to give up the management of the "Corner" into other hands, after being connected with it for thirteen years. The Guild owes a large debt of gratitude to Miss

Sharp for her labours, which were anything but light during all these years.* On Miss Sharp's retirement Mrs. Vaughan Nash was appointed by the Committee

MRS. VAUGHAN NASH.

of the *News* to take her place, and Miss Webb's help was obtained for a time to deal with the difficult mass of Guild communications. Mrs. Nash had already been

---

* Miss Sharp's work for women Co-operators did not end there, for she held the post of Vice-President of the Guild for five years, and contributed some of the most used papers to the Guild Library—"What has a woman to do with Co-operation?" "How to conduct branch elections," &c. Miss Sharp was also President of the Rugby Branch, and as early as 1887 was elected on to the Committee of the Coventry District Association.

connected with the Guild for ten years, and had complete sympathy with and knowledge of its work and aims. She has been inseparably associated with the present writer during the whole of their Co-operative life—a period now of over twenty years. Of her unseen work, as friend and counsellor, it is not possible here to speak. To the Guild she is known as the writer of many pamphlets,* as the Editor of the "Corner," and reporter of the Guild Annual Congresses. Her articles on Guild meetings and publications are some of the best records the Guild possesses.

Although from the beginning, there is a similarity of subjects, treatment, and views, the special tastes and bent of each Editor have stamped themselves to a large extent on the "Woman's Corner." The progress of the Guild has also been reflected in the "Corner," where members have found information and advice not only on domestic affairs but also on industrial and national questions.

* "Women as Consumers;" "Co-operative Production and the Needs of Labour;" "Life and Death in the Potteries;" "Hours of Employment for Women;" "The Law relating to Health in Factories and Workshops;" "Accidents Compensation Act;" "Notes on Tolstoy's Opinions."

H

CHAPTER VIII.

KINDRED GUILDS—FOREIGN INTERCOURSE.

A NY record of the movement to organise English women Co-operators would be incomplete without mentioning the Guilds which have sprung up in other countries.

The Scottish Co-operative Women's Guild, started in 1892, has made sturdy progress on its own lines, and now numbers 82 branches, 11 districts, and 7,153

SCOTTISH AND DUTCH DELEGATES AT LINCOLN
CONGRESS, 1908.

members. The relations existing between the two Guilds are of the friendliest character. The members of the Scottish deputation, at our Congresses, are always welcome visitors, and their eloquent and humorous speeches have contributed much to the success of our gatherings. Co-operative visits have also been paid by English officials to Scotland. The Scottish women have joined hands with the English women in vigorous protests against the sugar and bread taxes, and sent a warmly sympathetic letter to the English Free Trade Demonstration in the Free Trade Hall, Manchester.

MADAME TREUB (President of the Amsterdam Branch of the Dutch Guild).

Attached to the Scottish Guild are nine Irish branches, which will, we hope, send some representatives this year to our Guild Congress.

None who were present at the Co-operative Congress at Liverpool, in 1899, will forget the ovation given by the delegates to Madame Treub, who

accompanied her husband, Professor Treub, one of
the Dutch representatives from Amsterdam. Madame
Treub spoke English, among many other languages,
fluently. She threw herself with enthusiasm into
learning every detail about the work and organisation
of the English Guild, so as to be prepared to start a
sister Guild in Holland. This she has done with
marked success. Miss Mayo, who was paying a visit
to Amsterdam, gave an account in the "Woman's
Corner" of the second meeting, which was held in
November, 1900. She wrote:—

"The little room first used at 'Ons Huis' was already too
small for the number who wished to come, and as no other
suitable place could be found, the Guild met in two detachments
on two consecutive nights at Madame Treub's house, some thirty
people coming in all. Two of the first 'jevrows' (women) to
appear wore the national head-dress—a gold helmet, covered
with lace, looped up over the forehead with gold buttons and long
pendants. The others were dressed just as Guild members would
be in England, and until they spoke might all have passed for
English. . . . After a little while I was asked to speak, and
Professor Treub interpreted what I said sentence by sentence.
I told of the growth of the movement in Britain, and what it had
done for the people. A soft chorus of 'Ja, ja, ach, ja,' at various
points showed that the evils of credit trading, cheap cutting shops,
and under-paid work are known in Holland as well as on this side
of the water. Then Madame Treub gave an earnest little address,
which was translated to me, and said she hoped I would tell the
English Guild members that their Dutch sisters were beginning
slowly to wake up and hoped to follow their example."

It was a great pleasure to welcome last year to the
Guild Congress at Lincoln two Dutch Guild ladies.
Miss Hugenholtz came as the representative of the
branch at Amsterdam, and Miss Bergsma of the branch
at the Hague. They were women of wide ideas, and

their presence and speeches contributed greatly to the interest of the Congress.

A French "Ligue" has also been formed in Paris, with Madame Robert-Halt as President, and Madame Guébin as Secretary. The formation was due to the "Comité Central de l'Union Co-operative des Sociétiés

MISS BERGSMA (President of the Hague
Branch of the Dutch Guild).

Françaises de Consommation," of which M. Charles Gide is President, the actual promoters being M. Daudé-Bancel (the General Secretary) and two other gentlemen.

Foreigners learnt something of the English Guild at the International Co-operative Congress at Manchester in 1902, where Miss Mayo was indefatigable as an interpreter and distributor of Guild literature. M. Héliés, one of the French delegates, included an account of the Guild in his report of the Congress.

A Guild was also started in Jamaica in 1903, but no news of it has so far been forthcoming.

No organisation has been formed, as yet, in Germany, but three German ladies—the late Frau Schwerin and Frauleins Simon and Jastrow—have been present at Guild Congresses, and afterwards written vivid and amusing descriptions for German and English newspapers. Among other foreign visitors to Guild meetings have been a Polish gentleman, M. Lzukiewicz, and the celebrated German Socialist, Herr Eduard Bernstein, who wrote, in 1900, two long and appreciative articles in the "Wochen-Bericht," a paper issued by the German Co-operative Wholesale Society. The first article dealt with the constitution of the Guild, and the second with the various social questions taken up by the Guild, the scheme of "Co-operation in Poor Neighbourhoods" receiving his warm approval. He says he is not afraid that Co-operative women will go too fast—they stand for progress. If occasionally enthusiasm carries us beyond the bounds of the immediately practical, so much the better, for our danger lies rather in stagnation and selfishness than in ill-considered hurry of reform.

Individuals in Italy, Russia, Belgium, the United States, California, Australia, Canada, and New Zealand have all been supplied with information and papers about the Guild. Professor Meneghelli (Bologna), Professor Varley (Ghent), Professor Somogysmano (Buda Pesth), and Professor Oseroff (Russia) have brought out pamphlets in which some account of the Guild has been given, while Guild literature has been requested for the Public Libraries of Sydney (Australia), New York and St. Louis (U.S.A.), for an Economic Association in Liège, a Società Umanitaria in Milan, an American Institute of Social Service, and the Musée Social of Paris.

CHAPTER IX.

THE GUILD AND THE LABOUR MOVEMENT.

WE have already pointed out how Guild women came gradually to see what far-reaching consequences were bound up with their "basket power." Loyalty to the Store meant also loyalty to the best interests of labour, so that the Store was thus seen to be an important factor in the labour movement. "The Store is the social market where wage-spending is henceforth to assume an intelligent position, not a merely blind or hostile one, towards wage-earning; where the significance of 'beating down' on the wholesale or retail scale will be realised; where the two forces of industrial organisation—the producers and the consumers—will join hands for giving greater security to the improved health and comfort, the better surroundings, and the brighter prospects which are expressed in the phrase 'Standard of Life.'" *

"We are all buyers," says Miss Clementina Black, in a paper she wrote for the Guild, "and it is our interest to buy our goods as cheap as we honestly can.

---

* "Unionism in the Workshop and the Store," by Vaughan Nash.

But it is not our interest to buy goods cheap by giving low wages to those who produce them."

It was clearly to the interest of all Co-operators (men and women) to be trade unionists, and all trade unionists (men and women) to become Co-operators, for the position of labour in demanding good conditions, would be greatly strengthened if Co-operators boycotted sweated goods, by purchasing at the Stores only trade union and fairly-made goods.

CO-OPERATION AND TRADE UNIONISM.

Such ideas gradually permeated the Guild, and led in 1891 to the first small labour campaign, so to speak, which was organised by the Guild. A resolution was passed by the Central Committee to the effect that a special effort be made to take our work among trade unionists' wives and women trade unionists, so as to show them (1) the value of the dividend, and (2) the benefits to labour resulting from Co-operative shopping.

The campaign began with a correspondence in the *Trade Unionist*,* where a letter appeared, entitled "Can women raise their husbands' wages?" This was accompanied by a letter from the General Secretary of the Guild, proposing that a series of conferences should be held between trade unionists, Co-operators, and their wives to promote the alliance between the two movements. The Women's Guild had obtained its credentials for bringing them together from a resolution passed

---

* Edited by Mr. Vaughan Nash.

at a joint conference of some leading trade unionists and Co-operators on November 6th, 1891.*

Special handbills were issued, and ten meetings were held.† They were only fairly attended, some very poorly; but at all a spirited discussion took place. Grievances were aired and misconceptions shown up, and an impetus given to the good feeling which has continued to grow between the two bodies.

The idea of a trade union label, such as had already been instituted in America, for goods made under union conditions, was started at these meetings, and the following resolution was passed: " That it is desirable that all purchasers at Stores should have the means of readily ascertaining that the goods they purchase there have been made under fair conditions, .

---

* "That we cordially recommend trade unionists and Co-operators to attend the joint trade unionist and Co-operative meetings now being organised in London and the neighbourhood by the Women's Co-operative Guild, with the view of promoting an alliance between the two movements.

(Signed),

F. C. BAUM (Executive London Trades Council).
F. MADDISON (Editor *Railway Review*).
BEN TILLETT (Dockers' Union).
TOM MANN (Amalgamated Society of Engineers).
BENJAMIN JONES (Co-operative Union).
G. SUTHERLAND (Co-operative Wholesale Society).
THOS. E. WEBB (Co-operative Wholesale Society).
J. J. DENT (Co-operative Union)."

† The meetings were addressed by Messrs. Parnell (Amalgamated Society of Joiners), Hey (Engineers), Tillett (Dockers), Sellicks (Engineers), Mann (Engineers), Clem Edwards (Shipping Trades), the late Tom Mc.Carthy (Dockers), V. Nash, H. Tait (Railway Servants), Arnold (Engineers), H. Orbell (Dockers), Sidney Webb, Maddison; Mrs. Ben Jones, Miss Tournier, Miss Spooner, Miss Llewelyn Davies, Miss May Abraham (Mrs. H. J. Tennant), and Miss Clementina Black; Messrs. Gardiner, Dent, Sutherland, Macleod, Hines, Powell, Wilson, and Webb. In addition to the special joint meetings, seven District Conferences were held, and Mr. Nash's paper, "Trade Unionism   Workshop and Store," was discussed at eight Societies.

and, with this object, suggests 'that such goods should be marked with a trade union label.'

WHY BUY SWEATED GOODS AND SUPPORT SWEATING FIRMS?

All TRADE UNIONISTS and their Wives should lay out their money at the

CO-OPERATIVE UNIONIST STORES,

436, COMMERCIAL ROAD,
227, BOW ROAD,
70, BRUNSWICK ROAD, POPLAR.

WHY?

1 Because the articles are good, and made under fair conditions. Let women boycott bad employers by refusing to buy their goods.

2 Because women can thus raise their husbands' wages. The Stores are managed by working people, who all share in the profits. For every £1 spent there, each Member gets 1s. as his or her share in the profits.

3 Because at the Stores you have a Free Library, Free Classes, Free Entertainments, etc.

Women's help is wanted in the Labour Movement.
Women must rally together and help on the good time coming by joining the Women's Co-operative Guild.
Women are the purchasers. They must be Co-operators.
Women also want help themselves. They need less work, more change, more to spend, more to read, more interests.
Come and give a hand, and see how the Guild can help you, as any or all of the following Meetings:

THURSDAY, FEB 18th, at 6 o'clock, in the CO-OPERATIVE HALL, Johnson Street, Commercial Road, Joint Social Evening for Tower Hamlets, Bow, and Poplar Branches. Music and Singing. ADDRESS by Miss LLEWELYN DAVIES (General Secretary, Women's Co-operative Guild) DIALOGUE between Mrs. STONE and Mrs. SHOFFER.

TOWER HAMLETS MEETINGS, at Toynbee Hall, Commercial Street, at 8 p.m.
MONDAY, MAR. 7 —DIALOGUE between Mrs. STONE and Mrs. SHOFFER.
MONDAY, MAR. 21 —ARGUMENT : " Must Women always be Household Drudges " ?

BOW MEETINGS, at the Stores, 227, Bow Road, at 8 p.m.
WEDNESDAY, FEB. 24 —DIALOGUE : " Must Women always be Household Drudges " ?
WEDNESDAY, MAR. 9 —ADDRESS by Miss TOURNIER (Vice-President of the Women's Co-operative Guild), on " How Women can help in the Labour Movement " ?
WEDNESDAY, MAR. 23 —DISCUSSION : " Is it worth while to join the Women's Guild " ?

POPLAR MEETINGS, at the Stores, 70, Brunswick Road, Poplar, at 2 30
MONDAY, FEB. 22 —DISCUSSION : " For and Against the Women's Guild."
MONDAY, MAR. 7 —ADDRESS by Mrs. JONES (President of the Women's Co-operative Guild).
MONDAY, MAR. 21 —DIALOGUE " Must Women always be Household Drudges " ?

The matter was put into the hands of a joint Sub-Committee of the Parliamentary Committees of the two

movements, and supported at their Congresses. The
only union to take action in the matter was the Felt
Hatters and Trimmers' Union. They issued a label

which was adopted by 60 per cent of the hat manu-
facturers. Guild branches were immediately cir-
cularised, and urged to push the stocking of labelled

hats in the Store. A Co-operative Manager, having
noticed the advertisement in the *News*, wrote at once
asking for a supply. The firm replied they were not
sure if they could supply them, the Masters' Association not having made up its mind what action to
take. The Manager wrote again, and said in that case
he must place his custom elsewhere, when a consign-
ment of labelled hats was the speedy result.

In August, 1894, we were pleased to receive the
following vote of thanks from the Secretary of the
Hatters' Union (Mr. Wilde):
"At our Quarterly Council
Meeting the best thanks of
the meeting were ordered
to be conveyed to you for
the splendid and admirable
way in which you helped to
diffuse the hat label among
your members." We hear
from the present Secretary
that the label has been of
great service. He also says:

HATTERS' UNION LABEL.

"It is not used in ladies' hats, as employers find no
demand for it." It will be for the Guild to create this
demand, and to look for the label not only inside the
lining of their husbands' hats, but of their own.

THE COAL WAR.

In the same year (1894) occurred one of the greatest
labour struggles that we of this generation have seen.

No greater proof could possibly have been given to trade unionists of the desirability of the alliance for which the Guild had just been working. It would be interesting if a record had been compiled, of the assistance rendered by Co-operative Societies during the lock-out. Our members helped in many ways. Some took in the children of starving families; others helped Relief Committees, distributed Co-operative flour tickets, and gave away clothing. As women, we rejoice in the part which was played by women, some employers going so far as to say that the men would have gone in at a reduction, if it had not been for the women. They endured with uncomplaining fortitude, identifying themselves entirely with the men in the struggle. Mrs. Knott (of Parkgate, Sheffield), one of the Central Committee, was most active in work. Miss Webb and Miss Spooner both visited affected districts, and sent accounts to the " Woman's Corner." Miss Spooner wrote :—

"Though the very houses had been sold over their heads, and they had neither money, furniture, nor food, not one showed the slightest sign of giving way. 'We've only been getting 15s. a week; how can we take a reduction on that and live? We'd sooner clem playing than clem working, if clem we must.'"

Some of these were Guild members, notably Mrs. Dickenson (of Leeds), who was then Secretary for the Airedale district. She addressed seven mass meetings in the neighbourhood of Leeds, and those who heard her at the great gathering in St. James's Hall, London, on November 7th, would remember the enthusiasm her eloquence called forth. Writing of it herself, she says :—

"It was at that time that I understood the true meaning of Co-operation, and especially the Women's Co-operative Guild. When I got to St. James's Hall and saw so many I knew, and from whom I received such kindly welcome, I fully understood the power of the Guild. . . . I did not see the London audience, but the starving women and children on whose behalf I had come to speak."

Miss Sharp, as Editor of the "Woman's Corner," appealed week by week, with encouraging words, for a fund for the women and children, and succeeded in raising over £45, while Mrs. Dickenson acknowledged another sum of £10 which Guild members and other Co-operators had sent her.

LABOUR LEGISLATION.

Although the great bulk of Guild members are married women, whose home is their "workshop," there are a large number who themselves work in the mills, and the great majority are connected in some way with factory or workshop life. It is natural, therefore, that the Guild should use its organised strength on behalf of women workers, in trying to secure better factory and workshop legislation.

When the Factory Bill of 1894 was introduced, the Guild forwarded memorials to the Home Secretary, asking that provision should be made to guard against the evils of sweating, by (1) compulsory registration of workshops, and (2) making the giver-out of work responsible for the conditions under which such work is done ; and also asking for the total inclusion of laundries, for the better protection of the women and girls. The Bill failed to get through in the session it was introduced, and improvements were incorporated on its being reintroduced. An additional memorial was sent by branches in London and the neighbourhood to the nine London M.P.'s who sat on the Grand Committee for dealing with the Bill, asking that provision should be made for the total abolition of overtime for women in the dressmaking, millinery, and tailoring trades.

At one period it seemed probable that a clause for the raising of the age of half-timers would be introduced into the Bill. Now, though the Central Committee and the majority of branches were in favour of this rise, large numbers of our members, who were directly affected, in Lancashire and Yorkshire, held different views. So an expression of opinion from Lancashire and Yorkshire branches was sought, but only 17 responded out of about 60. Nine passed resolutions in favour of raising the age, óne approved without a resolution, and seven were opposed. At the Annual Congress that year the subject was treated in a paper by a former weaver (Mrs. Rigby, of Bury), and an interesting discussion took place.

"Speaker after speaker—for the most part women to whom the inside of a factory is as familiar as the outside—stood up in favour not only of raising, but abolishing the half-time system. The other side of the question—the welcome addition of the children's earnings—was also dealt with, one delegate remarking that she should never forget the first time her daughter brought in her first week's wage. 'The 2s. 4d.' she said, 'seemed to go further than a sovereign had done previously.' But this view of the question found little sympathy ; and the majority of the speakers told how, though sorely pressed, they had refused to take advantage of the half-time system, and urged the necessity of mothers

making the sacrifice necessary to give their children an education
which shall fit them, physically, morally, and intellectually, to
take their places as the citizens of the future."—*Co-operative News
Supplement.*

Lancashire women rebutted with some show of
feeling, the idea put forward by others, that "all the
vices were found bottled up in a factory." The resolution in favour of raising the age to 12 was carried with
only four or five dissentients.

At this annual meeting a resolution was passed
approving the 1894 Factory Act, but regretting the
exclusion of laundries and the non-abolition of overtime. As soon as this Act was passed, the Central
Committee set to work to explain its operation to the
members, and to educate and gain their opinion on the
further reforms needed. Papers were written sum-
marising the law, and suggesting improvements on
hours, overtime, home work, and the number of women
factory inspectors. Great interest was aroused by these
papers, which were read by 150 of the 200 branches,
and resolutions were sent in by 82 branches.

Information was also collected through the branches
regarding non-textile conditions of work, so as to obtain
more complete knowledge, and to strengthen our case
for reforms. The result of all this work was to set
out a programme of the reforms the Guild desired,
which were summed up in resolutions passed at the
annual meeting, at Burnley, 1896. These were :—

(1) Reduction of non-textile hours to those of textile
    trades.

(2) Further restriction and ultimate abolition of
    overtime for women.

I

(3) Inclusion of laundries under Factory Acts.

(4) Replacement of home by factory work.

(5) Increase in number of women factory inspectors.*

(6) Appointment of women as certifying surgeons.

(7) Annual examination of the health of factory, children.

In May, 1900, a storm of indignation was roused among workers by the extraordinary proposals introduced by the Government in a new Factory Bill.† The Guild, at the instigation of the Women's Trade Union League, joined vigorously in the protest. "Workers! take steps to protect your interests," began a circular issued to branches, which were asked to act at once, and hold meetings, and flood the Home Office and M.P.'s with resolutions. Branches did not fail to respond. A specially good meeting was held at Grimsby, organised jointly by the Guild and Educational Committee. Posters appeared all over the town— " Danger ahead! This Bill, if carried into law, means the enslavement of women and children and the workers of this country, leaving them at the mercy of the Home Secretary, and for the first time legalises factory work on Sunday. Workers! maintain your privileges and Sunday's rest." After one month's existence the ill-starred Bill was withdrawn, and the new Bill, introduced in 1901, contained none of the old objectionable features.

---

* This was again brought forward at the annual Congress in 1898, and a woman inspector for the Potteries was recommended at the Congresses in 1898 and 1899.

† The principal proposals dealt with a two-shift system, increased power for the Home Secretary, overtime, and freedom for laundries from regulations.

Again and again, the Guild has passed resolutions urging regulations as regards the hours and conditions under which shop assistants work.   The Guild's policy is that of the Union of Shop Assistants, which urges compulsory closing, and regulation of meal hours and general conditions.   These points are embodied in Sir C. Dilke's Bill, as opposed to the permissive Bill of Lord Avebury.

An extremely interesting conference was held in April, 1897, when Miss Reddish read a paper on "Accidents and Compensation," at Doncaster.   Her own experience of factory life and its accidents made her statements of great weight, and in the discussion which followed nearly all the speakers brought forward cases of terrible hardship inflicted on the worker.* Miss Reddish maintained that nothing short of compulsory compensation for all accidents by the employer would meet the case.   She showed by a diagram how large a proportion of accidents were "nobody's fault." Every injured workman was entitled to payment for his loss of wages.   This was a burden it was only fair to require industry to bear through the employer.

During the months following on this conference, a most important Bill (The Workmen's Compensation Bill) was going through Parliament.   This established the principle of compensation for all injuries, for which

---

* Examples: At Hindley, three years before, the front of a boiler blew out and killed a boy. The father took the case into court, and asked for £50. He got nothing, and was discharged. A girl fell down a hoist, and was killed. The firm paid for the funeral. A machine tool maker at Halifax had to have his arms amputated to the elbows. His wages for three months were paid by the firm, and a public subscription raised him £1,000.

I

Miss Reddish had contended—an immense advance on the old law embodied in the Employers' Liability Act.

At the annual Congress that year (1897) Mrs. Vaughan Nash read a paper explaining the points of the new Bill, and our members showed the keenest interest. There was no sensationalism in the manner the speakers recounted their terrible experiences; and prevention, rather than compensation, was naturally what speakers felt essential.

The Bill, as is known, is now law; and, limited as it is, is of the greatest importance to the workers in the establishment of a principle.

Any account of the labour work of the Guild would be incomplete without mentioning the efforts made to secure the sale of leadless-glaze pottery and non-poisonous matches. Among the methods adopted have been lectures at branches, pressure on Store Committees, shows of sample leadless pottery, distribution of pamphlet by Mrs. Nash on "Life and Death in the Potteries," and resolutions supporting stringent measures in manufacture.

It will thus be seen that the Guild is seeking freedom and health for the workers by means of legislation in their best interests, which should be the interests of all. But no women's labour policy can be fully effective without the power to vote for legislators who will carry out their wishes.

When the new Labour Department of the Board of Trade was established, in 1893, the Guild offered its

help in collecting information about women.   Miss
Collet (the correspondent for the Women's Section)
arranged that the first inquiry should be made into the
number, ages, and occupations of our married members.
6,500 schedules were sent out to our branch Secretaries.
A good deal of heart-burning was occasioned, but 757
answers were sent in, and out of these 314 expressed
willingness to give further information.

. A more continuous piece of work was started in
1894.   Ever since May of that year, Miss Reddish has
been forwarding monthly returns, for the *Labour
Gazette* under the title of "The State of Women's
Employment." The object is to give information as
to the amount and regularity of employment in the
textile trades, and for this purpose correspondents are
sought in different towns and districts.   In the first
year there were 33 correspondents, of whom 29 were
Guild members.   The number gradually increased,
till now it is 57, of whom 24 are Guild members.

In June, 1894, Mrs. Ashworth made a special
investigation in Burnley, into the conditions under
which children were left when their mothers went out
to work in the mills.   The results were published in
the *Labour Gazette*, June, 1894 :—

"Out of 165 cases covered by the inquiry, 39 children were
left with grandparents, 20 with elder sisters or housekeepers,
3 with the father, 24 with other relatives, and 70 with neighbours.
In the remaining 9 cases, the children were left with none to take
care of them."

CHAPTER X.

THROUGH CO-OPERATION TO CITIZENSHIP.

"THE duties of Co-operators as citizens" is a well-known phrase in the movement; and though women are still deprived of the right of citizenship, this has not prevented Guild women from learning citizens' duties, and performing them as far as they are able. We believe that Co-operation has its relation to the Municipality and State as well as to industrial organisations, and our members greatly appreciate this view. They remark on the much narrower scope of other women's associations, and say that the Guild "differs from other bodies, in extending our points of view; we are not narrowed down to one subject, or even one set of subjects." Again—"Old narrow ways of thinking have given way to broader views of life. I formerly held the view that there was no need for me to have a vote, but I have now come to the conclusion that human responsibility cannot be taken by another. It was a long step from such a narrow view of women's duties, to believing that women ought not only to vote but to take part in the administration of the law, so far as they were allowed." (This member is now a Poor-Law Guardian.)

The public work which is most easily within the reach of Guild members is that of Poor-Law Guardians. The subject was first brought before the Guild at the Doncaster Congress in 1894, when Mrs. Abbott (Tunbridge Wells) read a paper, which was taken back for discussion at branch meetings. Great interest was aroused, conferences were held, and Guild members urged to stand as Poor-Law Guardians. The local elections took place in December, 1894, when 45 members of the Guild were among the candidates, of whom 22 were successful, about 14 of these (though not all working women) standing in consequence of the Guild's agitation. Amongst these were Mrs. Bury* (President of Darwen Branch) and Mrs. Hodgett (President of Lincoln Branch), who have continued to sit till the present time, having thus served ten years. No women had previously sat on either the Blackburn or the Lincoln Union. Mrs. Bury says:—

"Men bitterly resented this advent of women in their special preserves. This has been lived down, and expressions such as 'I don't know what we should do without our women Guardians' are often heard. At a ward meeting, called to choose candidates, an Alderman said he was in favour of putting another woman in, for he was convinced in his own mind that they made the best Guardians. One of the Guardians is rather deaf, and in describing his difficulty in following the business through this defect he said, 'I watch the women and see how they do, and I'm never far wrong.' This is all the greater compliment as he holds political views opposite to our own. . . . Before women sat on our Board all girls with sad histories had to come *alone* before a large body of men. Now, after I had pleaded with the Board and got a resolution passed, the women Guardians and matron deal with the cases in a separate room."

---

* Also Mrs. Dickenson, the miner's wife, of Leeds.

How well Mrs. Bury's services have been appreciated, is seen from the fact of her having been made Chairman of the large and important Infirmary and Lunacy Committee, and she was also selected to open a new wing to the Infirmary buildings.

MRS. HODGETT.

Much the same experience befell Mrs. Hodgett, in the Lincoln Union. On first standing, the Vicar of the parish opposed her nomination, but on the last occasion, the Churchwarden sent her the paper filled in, without solicitation. When first elected, the Chairman

of the Board invited the women into the Board-
room to make their acquaintance and explain some of
their duties. He openly expressed his disapproval,
and said he would be like the boy with the physic—
make the best of it. He was very anxious as to
whether the women would wish to speak sitting down,
and was much reassured when they said "No." Mrs.
Hodgett says:—

"Years after, on his retirement, he confessed to his conversion,
and bore generous testimony to the good work of the women, and
the way they always spoke to the point. . . . When it was
first proposed to send women to Poor-Law Conferences, a cry was
raised at the Board, 'Let the women stay at home and cook their
husbands' dinners.' Since then, for three years in succession, I
was elected as one of two representatives to the Central Poor-Law
Conference, and am the first woman to be appointed Chairman
of the Nursing Committee, and Vice-Chairman of the House
Committee."

Year after year the subject of Poor Law has been
before the Guild. In 1895 it was taken at all our
Sectional Conferences. In 1896 a special campaign
was organised in preparation for the elections in
April. It was made the principal subject in the
Winter Circular. Four papers were published,[*] 105
branches studied the question, three reading parties
and a correspondence class were held, and many
visits were paid to Workhouses. The result was that
the number of our Guardians was increased to 36,
and only six candidates failed. At the elections both
in 1898 and 1901, branches worked energetically
for women candidates, Guild members or otherwise

---

* (1 and 2) "History of Poor Law," by Miss Bompas (Leeds).
  (3 and 4) "Poor-Law Administration," by Miss Booth (Liverpool).

In the elections which have just taken place (April, 1904), 81 Guild members were returned as Guardians, eight of whom headed the polls in their respective wards or towns.   Among these was Mrs. Deans, of Plumstead, one of the earliest Woolwich members, and President of the Guild in 1899.

In 1897 we took up the subject of Public Health Laws, and were most fortunate in obtaining the services of Miss Alice Ravenhill (A.S.I.), who in five months gave 71 lectures to 20 Societies.   The attendances were excellent, and Miss Ravenhill had the power of holding her audiences.   As one of the hearers said, she "brought in no three-and-sixpenny words," and she made each feel that public health was a matter of personal interest.   Interest in the lectures was increased by a series of coloured diagrams. One of these was a large tree showing the machinery for making and carrying out the Health Laws; others gave statistics about vaccination and death rates; another was a picture of a notoriously unhealthy village, in which the churchyard was placed above the village at the top of a hill, thus polluting the water supply, where the houses were hovels, against which heaps of refuse were piled, while the tattered children showed the demoralising effect of the surroundings. "I was not going to stand any more smells when I knew how to get rid of them," said a Guild woman after one meeting, so she went to the Sanitary Inspector. The next morning all the dust-bins in her row of cottages were cleared, and by three o'clock the inspector had visited all the tenants, to say what was and what

was not, to be thrown in.   On one branch sending up
a list of questions to the local Health Committee the
Mayor said—"If we give in to this kind of thing we
may have to answer questions from Timbuctoo and
Tasmania."   Nevertheless the Town Clerk was directed
to obtain the required information.

Besides these lectures, many others were given by
Medical Officers of Health, Sanitary Inspectors, and
others.   The campaign was supplied with powder and
shot in the shape of seven specially written penny
pamphlets on Public Health.* Such work was naturally
followed up by similar campaigns on the Housing
Question in (1898 and 1899),† and the Land Question
in 1901.‡

A great injustice was done to women when the
London Government Act of 1899 was passed, by which
Vestries, on which women had had a right to sit, were
abolished, and Borough Councils instituted, from which
women were expressly excluded.   The Women's Local
Government Society urged the Guild to protest before

---

* These pamphlets were "Health of the Community," by Miss Ravenhill;
"The Law Relating to Nuisances," by Miss E. A. Bompas; "Drains and
Dustbins," also "The Law Relating to Infectious Diseases," by Miss R.
Macmillan "The Prevention of Smoke," by Miss L. Harris; "The Housing
of the People," by Mrs. Phillimore; "The Law Relating to Health in
Factories and Workshops," by Mrs. V. Nash.

† Eighty-five lectures were given at 52 branches, and seven new penny
pamphlets published :—"How the Law Helps to Healthy Homes," also "Our
Water Supply," by Miss Ravenhill; "The Housing of the Working Classes Act,
1890," also "Municipalities and Housing Reforms," by the late Dr. Bowmaker;
"The Housing of the People," by Mrs. Phillimore; "Co-operative House
Building," by Miss Mayo; "House Furnishing," by Miss Dowson.

‡ Conferences were held to discuss a paper by Mrs. Abbott, on "The Claim
of the People on the Land," and lectures and addresses given.

the final voting on the Bill.* But the reactionary forces prevailed, and all we could do was to record our indignation at our Congress at Plymouth, in 1900, at women being deprived of an already existing right to civic service, and to suggest that all women's organisations should unite to promote a Bill to enable women to sit on County and Town Councils.

A Bill to this effect is now before Parliament, but where are any signs of grace? For the present Government has calmly continued its policy of depriving women of their rights, in its recent Education Act (1902). As is well known, this Bill abolished School Boards—on which women, equally eligible with men, had done good work—and created Educational Committees (of Town and County Councils), to which women were only allowed admission by co-optation.† All protests, from men and women alike, were unavailing, and a third injustice to women is now threatened, rumour says, namely, that of depriving women of the right of popular election to Boards of Guardians, by making their work also part of the work of Town and County Councils.

---

* The following circular was issued to the Guild branches:—"The Central Committee feel sure your branch will agree in thinking a protest should be made against the injustice of taking from women the small rights they already possess and are using so well. If your members agree, please write to your local M.P.'s, calling attention to the excellent work women are doing on vestries, showing how important their co-operation is in public health and other matters, and ask them to be in their places in the House of Commons and vote for the complete eligibility of women."

† This was not the only reason for the opposition which the Guild expressed to the present Education Act. It disapproved of the control of education being put into the hands of a body not directly responsible to the ratepayers, and of the inadequate provision for higher secondary education.

But this treatment of women is not taking place without effect. Women have been roused, and they realise the weakness of their position without a vote. The result is that a wave of enthusiasm and determination has set in, and it is not improbable that these wrongs may prove to be blessings in disguise. Just as the labour party is gaining fresh life, owing to the threatened destruction of trade unions, so women (whose cause is so similar to that of labour) may find that measures of exclusion will lead to their ultimate freedom as citizens.

Other occurrences have also contributed to produce this awakening among women, especially among Co-operative women. Questions of taxation, leading to rises in the price of food, affect Co-operators and working women very closely indeed. The Guild began to take action in 1894, when, joining with Co-operative Societies, it forwarded a memorial to the Chancellor of the Exchequer in favour of what is known as a "Free Breakfast Table," urging the removal of taxes from tea, coffee, cocoa, chicory, and dried fruits. The policy laid down was subsequently followed up by vigorous petitions to Chancellors, resolutions to M.P.'s, and speeches by women on the proposed sugar* and corn duties, and culminated in the great protest

---

* An inquiry was made among certain Guild members as to the difference the proposed ½d. per lb. tax would make in their weekly expenditure. The amount of sugar used varied a good deal, according to the size of family, the ordinary amount being from 6lbs. to 10lbs. a week. The tax on this would mean an increased expenditure of from 8d. to 5d. a week. The Women's Trade Union League joined with the Guild in asking for a deputation (which was refused) to the Chancellor of the Exchequer.

K

that has been made by our members in favour of free trade, when the fiscal campaign of last year (1903), was sprung upon the country.

"In the campaign against the proposed fiscal changes the Women's Co-operative Guild, which has done more, perhaps, than any other organisation to educate the wives and daughters of industrial toilers of the country on social and economic questions, will play no mean part." So speaks a leading article in the *Co-operative News*. There was no doubt of the line which the Guild would take on this matter. The Congress at Lincoln last year (1903) gave the lead in no uncertain way. It expressed its "emphatic disapproval of any proposal for interfering with the policy of free trade by a system of preferential tariffs, which it believed would enrich monopolists, impoverish the people, corrupt public life, and embitter international relations." A few branches reported disagreement, but, taking it as a whole, the Guild has stood firm to the free trade policy, and has not been misled by specious arguments. A special paper, "The Necessity for Free Trade," was issued by the Guild, and discussed at conferences, while many branches arranged lectures from prominent free trade champions, among whom Mrs. Bury came to be included.

But it was felt that more than one of the ordinary Guild campaigns was needed at this crucial moment, and that something special was demanded from Co-operative women. So on October 10th, 1903, there appeared the following notice at the head of the

"Woman's Corner":—"The Guild is organising a great Free Trade Demonstration on November 11th, in the Free Trade Hall, Manchester." Then came an appeal to our members in the following words:—

"There has never been a national crisis when our members had more right to speak out or more claim to be heard. As Co-operators, women will see that the prosperity of the country depends on the spending power of the people, which would be decreased by high prices, consequent on taxation of food. And as chancellors of the family exchequers, women know best the importance of being able to make the money go as far as possible. A Co-operative mother is not likely to believe in taxing food, nor be duped by the suggestion that if taxes were taken off tea and tobacco, it would not signify if bread and meat were dear. In order that women may come in their thousands and uphold the Free Trade policy, we have engaged the Free Trade Hall, in Manchester, which is capable of holding 4,000 persons. . . . Let us show that Co-operative women can be roused, and make our voice heard throughout the length and breadth of the land."

Help was sought from Manchester women's associations, and with their co-operation a remarkable demonstration of women took place. The hall was decorated with Guild banners and free trade mottoes. Long before the beginning of the meeting, Guildswomen and others began to arrive, coming in large numbers from the surrounding towns. Labour and anti-Protection choruses, accompanied by the great organ, were sung, and excitement and expectancy were high when Mrs. Bury (the Chairman) led the way on to the platform, followed by a remarkable array of speakers and supporters representing nearly all shades of social and political opinion. The speakers were:.

Miss Garland (Women's Free Trade Union), Mrs. Cobden Unwin (daughter of Richard Cobden), Mrs. Booth (Co-operative Guild), Mrs. John Winbolt (weaver), Mrs. Byles (Salford), Mr. Ernest Beckett (Conservative, and Unionist Free Food League), Mr. Alfred Emmott (Liberal, and Free Trade Union), and Mr. Philip Snowden (Socialist). Very interesting letters of sympathy were read from prominent women—Lady Aberdeen, Lady Henry Somerset, Mrs. Henry Fawcett, Mrs. Bright Mc.Laren (John Bright's sister), Mrs. H. J. Tennant, &c. The speeches were excellent, and the audience alive to every point. The applause broke out again and again as speaker after speaker emphasised the need for the Parliamentary vote. The following resolution was carried unanimously :—

"That this meeting of women declares its steadfast adherence to the policy of Free Trade, and condemns all attempts to revive the system of Protection, which would impoverish the people, enrich monopolists, corrupt public life, and embitter colonial and international relations ; and seeing that women, both as workers and housewives, are so deeply concerned in this question, deplores that they cannot make their protest effective through being debarred from the Parliamentary franchise." ·

What greater impetus could have been given to the question of Women's Suffrage, with which this chapter will fittingly close, than the present fiscal crisis ? The agitation for the right of citizenship began and continued for many years almost entirely among middle-class women ; but a very marked change has come in this respect within recent years, and working women have now come forward to claim the vote, not only from the point of view of justice, but also because they see how closely the actual needs in their lives are connected with it.

In 1893, the leaders of the Women's Suffrage movement decided to promote an appeal to Members of Parliament, from women of all classes and parties, to show that the vote was more widely desired than was thought.   Books were issued for the collection of signatures.   The Guild contributed 2,225 names, and the Appeal Secretary, in her letter of thanks, said that the Co-operative women had worked splendidly.   Four years afterwards, in 1897, at the time when a Women's Suffrage Bill was before Parliament, the Guild took up the subject on its own account, and issued papers entitled, "Why Working Women Need the Vote," which were discussed at the Southern Sectional Conferences.

"After this month let us hear no more of 'Working women do not want the vote.' The tone throughout the meeting was most practical and sensible. Working women want to make themselves felt in public life for definite purposes—to improve the social laws and administration, and particularly to watch over the lives of women and children. To reject from the electorate public-spirited workers like these is a folly which nothing but voluntary ignorance can account for." *

Resolutions in support of the Suffrage Bill were enthusiastically passed. A few months later a letter, signed "A Guild Member," appeared in the "Woman's Corner," strongly condemning the attitude Mr. Broadhurst, M.P., had taken on this Bill, at a meeting of the National Liberal Federation, at Derby. Twenty-three branches proceeded to pass resolutions of protest,

---

* "Woman's Corner," *Co-operative News*, March 27th, 1897.

and these were forwarded to Mr. Broadhurst, whose reply was as follows :—

"MY DEAR MADAM,

    "I asked that those most fitted to vote, viz., married women and servant maids, should be included. I did not promise to vote for the Bill if they were included. I did not say I would vote against the Bill.
                                "Yours, &c.,
                                        "H. BROADHURST."

This letter is rather mysterious, and the necessity for the importunate widow's policy is obvious. Mr. Maddison (then M.P.) was also written to, concerning his remark at the Women's Liberal Federation meeting, that the only women who wanted votes were idlers or Tory bigots, and we wished to know under which head to place the thousands of our Co-operative women who desired to be voters.

In 1900 began a remarkable new move among the trade unionist women of the North, in which Guild members have taken some part. A monster petition, organised by the North of England Suffrage Society, was signed by 29,359 women cotton operatives in Lancashire, and presented to certain Members of Parliament at the House of Commons. Miss Reddish (President of Bolton Branch of the Guild) introduced the deputation, among whom were several Guild members. The following year the Yorkshire and Cheshire textile workers followed suit, with a petition signed by 31,000 women. Miss Reddish and seventeen Guild members were among the deputation to the Members of Parliament. In the short space of eleven months Lancashire, Yorkshire, and Cheshire women textile operatives contributed 68,000 signatures.

This work led on to further very interesting developments. Branches of the Weavers' Unions were asked to make Women's Suffrage a trade union question, and a Women's Suffrage candidate for Parliament has now been selected for Wigan, whose candidature is promoted by a special Labour Representation Committee of women, including members of the North of England Suffrage Society and textile workers. Out of the 29 on the Committee 13 are members of the Guild.

Thus we see Co-operative and trade unionist women each approaching the question of the Parliamentary suffrage, from their own special standpoints of workers and consumers, seeing more clearly every day the fundamental importance of the enfranchisement of women.

CHAPTER XI.

PERSONAL AND DOMESTIC.

THE members who form the Guild, are almost entirely married women belonging to the artisan class, and are associated, through their husbands and relatives, with all the prevailing trades of the localities in which the Guild branches are situated. We find husbands of Guild members among weavers, mechanics of every kind, miners, railway men, Co-operative employés, dock labourers, country labourers, bricksetters, printers, joiners; and every sort of miscellaneous tradesman and worker is included—cement and quarry workers, warehousemen, draymen, not omitting chimney sweeps, gardeners, painters, van-drivers, coachmen, &c. It will thus be seen that the Guild stands, as previously explained, for the organised purchasing or consuming power of the working-class community of the country.

As regards the Guild women themselves, a certain proportion, especially in Lancashire, work in the mills, while others go out to nurse, wash, clean, and some are teachers and dressmakers. But for the greatest number, their homes are their workshops.

The childhood recollections of many of the members are very interesting. For example, one of the Midland Guildswomen will relate how she was brought up in a Leicestershire village, one of a family of eleven, and used to

work in the fields; how her father was a shepherd earning
12s. a week, her mother sitting up late to seam hosiery,
which was brought in large cartloads from the town.
Another member writes how she worked in the fields
for four years in a gang of children, driven by a man
with a long whip. The pay was 4d. to 6d. a day.
"In harvest time we left home at four o'clock in the
morning, and stayed in the fields till it was dark.
Often, before and after work, there was a walk of two
to five miles. Many of the children entered the gang
at five years old. I never worked one hour under
cover of a barn, and only once did we have a meal in
a house. Often the whole gang would be crying with
the cold, and working while they cried." At the age of
twelve she began her factory life, as a full-timer in a
flax mill at Leeds. She says :—

"I had ten flights of steps to climb, morning, noon, and night,
to reach room No. 56, and it took me an hour to walk the distance
between my home and the factory. My wage was five shillings.
The difference between the pure air of the open fields and the
heat, the clouds of dust, and foul smells inseparable from this
trade soon played havoc with my health, so I left and went to
work in the spinning department of a large woollen factory,
notorious for its number of accidents. After staying two or three
years at spinning I became anxious to learn the weaving trade,
and I went to one of those factories where it was almost death
(physical and moral) to work. This factory was owned by church-
going people—people who were very prominent at opening bazaars
and heading subscription lists."

Amongst those who have been Presidents of the
Guild, one began work at eight years old, another was
a full-timer at ten, another began work as a "winder"
at six and a half, and another as a little servant
between ten and eleven. It may be of interest to

note that the husbands of our present Central Committee carry on the trades of engineer, organist,
carpenter, gasfitter (late), tailor, and manager of cotton
mill.   Of their wives, three were apprenticed to dressmaking (which they consider "slavery"), two were
heel-knitters in mills, and two were brought up to no
trade.

Connected with the Guild, as Editors of the
" Woman's Corner," as Organising Secretaries, and as
occasional Branch Presidents or Secretaries, have been
a few women who have had time—"that commodity
much needed by working women"—at their disposal, and whose sympathies attracted them to a
working-class organisation rather than to philanthropic
work.   But those who join the Guild take their place
on an equality with all, standing for election with the
rest, and winning their way if the members wish it.
They must identify themselves with working-class
interests, and come as interpreters of the needs and
wishes of the workers.   The Guild does not seek
outsiders of "position" to preside over its functions
or direct its councils.   On the contrary, it has been
suggested that a meeting of ladies of rank might be
organised, with addresses by working women, on the
hardships of dressmakers, shop assistants, and domestic
servants, and of the possibilities of life in one or two
rooms.

Some of the Guild families live in houses of their
own, which they have bought through Co-operative
or other Building Societies.   But the houses of the
great majority are rented at from 4s. to 7s. 6d. per

week, according to the locality and family earnings. The typical Guild home may be described as follows:— A two-storeyed house, with a narrow entrance passage, out of which opens on the right or left the "front room," the abode of treasures, photographs, perhaps a piano, where guests are hospitably entertained, and Sunday rests and reads taken. At the end of the passage is the kitchen, with its inviting polished fireplace, the real living-room of all, looking out into the back yard. Between the kitchen (out of which a small scullery opens) and the front room is a narrow, steep flight of stairs, at the top of which is a bedroom on either hand. Some of the houses will have a third bedroom; only a few have the luxury of a bathroom.

These homes are the workshops of many trades, where overtime abounds, and where an eight hours' day would be a very welcome reform, for it is a true saying that "a woman never knows when her day's work is done." Few men can realise how much drudgery and lonely effort there is in the everyday work of a housewife. If men need a life apart from their daily work, women need it equally. Leisure and time for matters other than domestic, are indeed wants in working women's lives, and it is astonishing how time is somehow made for Guild and other public work. "One of the things the Guild teaches, is system," says a member. "To be able to attend branch meetings and conferences, and do your household duties, you must have system in your home work. You can't loiter over it. The Guild really gives a zest to it." Another says: "You need to work very systematically, and it simply means, no matter how you feel, well or ill, everything must be done in order, or everything would get into a muddle."

Here are some specimens of the " system " adopted by Guild members :—

" MONDAY—Washing and ironing.
" TUESDAY—Tidying, sewing, preparing dinner for Wednesday.
" WEDNESDAY—Poor-Law day.
" THURSDAY—Bake, and clean bedrooms.
" FRIDAY—Clean rest of house, and have help for half a day.
" SATURDAY—Two or three hours of Poor-Law work."

This Poor-Law Guardian says :—

" I have had a splendid constitution, and the busy life suited me. Most of my lectures and addresses have been thought out when my hands have been busy in household duties—in the wash tub, when baking (and, by the way, I have never bought a week's baking during my married life of over twenty-one years), or doing out my rooms. Somehow the work passes more quickly, and I have not felt the work so hard when my mind has been filled with other things."

Or, this is how a Yorkshire woman manages :—

" MONDAY.—Washing. Guild at 7.
" TUESDAY.—Starching and ironing. Educational Committee at 7-30.
" WEDNESDAY.—Darning and sewing.
" THURSDAY.—Cleaning rooms. A Co-operative meeting.
" FRIDAY.—Baking and do kitchen.
" SATURDAY.—Cleaning and get clothes ready for wash."

A Southerner, living on the outskirts of a town in a six-roomed house, is not obliged to be "either a slut or a slave," as a Guildswoman remarked was the case in Sheffield, but she has a hard time of it, too.

" MONDAY.—I get up at twenty minutes to six and light fire in kitchen, then light fire for copper, and fill it with water. Then cook bacon, put dinners ready, and start off three, by twenty past six. Then, of course, water is warm, ready for washing. Do not clean up house, except breakfast things, till clothes are drying. Fold clothes, and come out to Nursing Class. Sometimes I can get mangling done in afternoon, if the clothes dry quickly.

"TUESDAY.—I iron up till dinner-time, make pies and cakes for men's dinners—jam pies, bacon pies, rabbit pies, meat pies. After dinner, I make cake for breakfast, cake for their dinner, cake for their tea; they'll eat cake nearly always.

"WEDNESDAY.—Finish my ironing, if I had extra lot, till dinner. Sewing Meeting, or running about for Guild.

"THURSDAY AND FRIDAY.—Turn out bedrooms, or a good big day of sewing. Stores Committee Meeting on Thursday, Guild on Friday.

"SATURDAY.—Touch up all round; hot dinner at one-thirty."

Lancashire women are as "house proud" as any, and certainly "system" is at the bottom of their success. One of these writes:—

"I arrange my home work each week, as follows: On Monday I clear up all rooms after Sunday, brush and put away all Sunday clothes, and then separate and put to soak all soiled clothes for washing. On Tuesday, the washing is done, the clothes folded and mangled. After the washing, the scullery receives a thorough cleaning for the week. Wednesday is the day for starching and ironing, and stocking darning, as well as the usual week's mending. On Thursday, I bake the bread and clean the bedrooms. On Friday I clean the parlour, lobby, and staircase, as well as the living-room. Saturday morning is left for all outside cleaning—windows and stonework—besides putting all the clean linen on the beds. I finish work on Saturday about 2 p.m., the rest of the day being free."

In addition to all the systematic work quoted above, there is always, of course, all the everyday work of preparing food, cleaning up, making beds, sending children to school, &c., &c.

A busy Guild Secretary, with a little family, confesses she keeps her housework at a minimum, trying to do all she can on the days when she has no Guild work, often baking, washing, and ironing on the same day. "On Sunday I often do most of my writing. Of course, some weeks things get thrown out of order, but I work them right again, and I find by having a big working week and a small one I can manage nicely."

An elderly Guild member writes as follows, with some humour:—

"Now I have a confession to make. I let it (house work) keep to a more convenient season, when it means a little more time to rid a little more dirt and dust and a few more microbes to kill, or a visit to a friend dispensed with. For the rest, paper writing and examination papers (for the Guild) I mostly do in the small hours of the morning, when otherwise I should be in bed, and I invariably rise at six o'clock, as I must have my husband's breakfast ready by seven. When I leave him for a Guild Congress I prepare plenty of food, and my son's wife looks in on him. He takes no harm—trust a man for that."

In the South, it is customary to buy bread, but, in spite of all the trouble of baking, Northerners will not usually do without their home-made loaves and cakes. Good Co-operative bread is making its way to some extent into the homes, but the old custom dies hard. As to washing-day, a good many women (and husbands, too) would gladly dispense with that. But the difficulty of the cost has not yet been solved. Perhaps in time Co-operative Societies with a large steady custom and good management will be able to institute Co-operative Laundries, where washing could be economically done (and under better conditions for the workers), and where holes would not be made in linen nor tapes and buttons torn off.*

With so much work, and so many lives depending on them, it is not surprising that we often find women who hardly ever leave their homes, whose lives become very monotonous and restricted, and whose spirits and health suffer severely. The testimonies of the health-giving properties of the Guild could almost rival those of Beecham's Pills. "I have come to Guild many times not knowing how I got there, I was that tired, but I felt stones weight lifted off my shoulders after. It has done more for me than either church or chapel work." "It has saved me from threatened melancholia," says another. "It brings me out" (in more than one sense) is what the Guild members say. Very few have the character and interest to study and think alone, unaided, in the way that the present writer found one woman in the Midlands was doing. She had read through the whole of Henry George's "Progress and Poverty" while she nursed her baby, and had herself written to the late William Morris to ask him to come and address a meeting in her village, and knew the writings of Edward Carpenter. She was a remarkable elderly woman, very plain and quiet in dress and manner, with plenty of critical power and

---

* While writing these pages an account has been received of a Laundry the Bradford Society has recently opened. The first week's trade was £30, and the last £100. Thirty-three persons are employed, most of whom are on piece work. Prices are very moderate, the cost of delivery being done away with. Members leave and fetch their linen at Branch Stores, the Society supplying hampers. Checks are given. The Laundry is considered a model in design and equipment.

A "Scottish Co-operative Laundry Association" at Barrhead is reported to be developing well, with an average trade of £95 a week.

wit. She took in *Justice* and *The Labour Prophet.*
" I should have gone melancholy," she said, " if I had
not had a bit of Socialism coming in each week." Her
husband was evidently very proud of her.

The majority of women need their interests stirred
from without, opportunities of taking part in a wider
life, and contact with others. And the Guild proves
every day that what it offers is just what certain
women want, however straitened (up to a certain
point) their means, and however large their families.
An ex-Guild President says :—

"I have found that it is not the wife of the fairly well-paid
mechanic who takes the greatest interest in Guild life generally,
but those whose incomes are from 20s. to 30s. a week; nor is it
those with small families, but more often those with large
families who are the most regular at branch meetings, most
loyal to Co-operative principles, and most willing to attend as
delegates to the various conferences."

The women say that the Guild has broadened their
minds, enlarged their ideas, and taught them to think
on social questions they would at one time have passed
over as outside their capacity. "A lot of our owder
women are sayin'," writes a member, "they wishes
Guild ud bin started while they were young, so as they
could have taken oud of o'th' advantages o' larning
th' Guild offers."

But what is so remarkable about so many of the
Guild members is that, although no longer young in
years, and having had little or no early advantages,
they possess a most youthful spirit, taking up new
ideas, attending lectures, writing papers, and throwing
themselves into a wider life with enthusiasm. The

following quotations from members show how the influence of the Guild makes itself felt:—

A Lancashire woman who was President of the Guild for two years says:—

"My school days were very few indeed. I went at the age of six to an old dame's school, kept in a cottage. I only went half time for six months. We learned to read one at a time, all from one book. One slate served for all the scholars, on which we made marks and letters; we were also taught to knit and sew. I left school when I was six and a half years old to commence work. At this time hand-loom weaving was the trade of the district, and children were employed in winding bobbins for the weavers from morning till night, the work being carried on in the homes of the people. This was the kind of work I did till I was twelve years of age; then I went to weave in a cotton mill, which was a better-paid trade."

Other members say:—

"I was the eldest of six children. Father at that time had only a small wage, so that I was sent to work at a pottery before I was nine years old. The schools that I attended were first an old dame's school, and then National School. So that it was very little that I learnt at school. It was at the Sunday School that I learnt to write. I remember so well the excitement that was aroused in our neighbourhood when it was stated that a branch of the Women's Guild was going to be started at ——. Several of us were very curious to know what it meant, so decided to go and see. I attended the second meeting, and have been a member ever since. I feel that it is entirely due to the Guild that my mind has been strengthened, and my views of life and things have been wider; and what it has done for me it is doing for others. As far as Co-operation went I was brought up in a Co-operative home, my father was a Director of the —— Society for a number of years, but all the work women could do then, apart from spending the money, was to attend the tea meetings and make tea occasionally. The advent of the Guild has changed all this. The Guild differs from other bodies that I know of in the variety of subjects considered at the meetings. Any subject occupying the public mind can be discussed."

L

"I think the Guild stands on a different footing from other organisations altogether. I think it broadens our minds, and makes us more thoughtful for others. I look on Co-operation as something better than even trade unionism in one way, because in trade unionism the workmen have to go to the employers to get a good wage, but in our movement we have it in our own power to give a good wage. If a woman belongs to the Guild she gets to think how things are made in a way she would not otherwise."

"To have no thoughts beyond one's home life does not seem to me to be the right thing, although home duties certainly occupy a great portion of a woman's life."

An unmarried Branch Secretary, who was a candidate at the last election of Poor-Law Guardians, confessed how the Guild made her realise her own ignorance :—

"When I became Secretary it was something of a shock to me to find out the extent of my own ignorance. In the matter of writing letters alone the Guild has been of immense value to me. Until I was Secretary I had not written half-a-dozen letters in my life, and, oh, what a trouble it was at first, and the quires of paper spoilt in the attempt."

This Secretary now writes some of the most interesting and best composed letters received at the Guild office.

The children of Guild members naturally benefit by wider ideas and work on the part of the women. "Since joining the Guild our women have seen to the better education of their children," writes a Branch Secretary, "and have made constant sacrifices to do this, and have succeeded in letting them stay longer at school."

"By goin' t'meetings, an' mixin' among folks (yer bun' to larn mure) aum better able to teach mi childer those things awf fun' out to be true. And it's made me feel a fitter mate for mi husband, becose when he comes whoam at neet un tells me what's goin' on i'th' town, au can harken an' raison back wi' him about things at consarns us ough."

So writes a Lancashire Branch President.

And what do the husbands say and feel about women becoming more than housewives? The feeling that a man is lord and master, and has a right to dictate and control the life of his wife, exists among Co-operative as well as other men. "So many men," says a Guildswoman, "think that women have no right to do anything outside their own wonderful abode." Cases are known where husbands prevent their wives attending the Guild meetings, because they are unwilling that their wives should be out, when they themselves are at home. Some women are strong and independent enough to take their own way, and win round their men folk. "I know one woman," says a Lancashire member, "whose husband would have prevented her going to the Guild, but she said, 'Nay, tha's had thy day in leaving me wi' childer, it's my turn nah, and ah's going.' I am happy to say he is now converted." Another husband did not like being left alone for the night when his wife went to conferences, "However, she attended three, and gets on very well with her chap now."

On the whole, active opposition is very rare, and it is pleasant to record that some of the Guild's warmest friends are the members' husbands. Of course, so noble a tyrant is not often to be found as one husband whose first wife was a Guildswoman. When he married again he gave his second wife no peace until she joined the Guild, in which she now takes great interest. One member represents her Guild branch on the Labour Electoral Committee of the town, and her husband is quite as anxious for her to improve as she is herself, and often jokes about her being their "Member of Parliament."

A husband will often stay at home willingly, while the wife has an evening's change from her ceaseless work; others take much interest in the Guild, helping with correspondence, and sometimes giving addresses at branch meetings. Many men much appreciate the sort of meetings the Guild carries on, and they have suggested more than once that a Men's Guild might be formed, because "if it could be kept on the same lines as the Women's is, it would be a benefit to Co-operation all round." In a conversation between two men after a Guild lecture, one was heard to remark, "I say, how don these women manage to get up sich good lecters? They're better nor moest o' thoose we getten fro' th' Educational Committee, an' th' women hanna so mich money for to goo at noather, but they beaten us chaps sometimes."

CHAPTER XII.

CONCLUSION.

"OF HOL HERTE COMETH HOPE."—*Vision of Piers Plowman*
(about 1370 A.D.).

FORMER chapters have shown the place which the Guild is taking in Co-operation, and how its Co-operative goal is full and real citizenship in the Co-operative State, so that women may serve as Co-operative citizens on terms of equality with men.

How, it may be asked, has the movement, as a whole, received the Guild and regarded its policy? It may be said with gratitude, that had it not been given generous recognition and sympathy, its position would not be what it is to-day.

But there has been, and still is, considerable prejudice to live down, and, though opposition is less openly expressed than it used to be, it is none the less strong in many quarters. It is especially roused when women see that there is something more for them to do than buy loyally at the Store, and proceed to demand open membership, to come forward for seats on Boards of Management, or stand for prominent positions in the movement. But opponents are gradually being won over, as they work side by side with women in the service of the movement; and Co-operative women need fear no set-back, if they remain united and resolute in their loyalty to the

Stores, to the policy of justice in employment, of truth in business dealings, and of fellowship in a common Co-operative life.

The other goal which all working women's organisations are bound to seek, is that of national citizenship. As soon as women are in earnest as regards industrial and social reform, they are inevitably led to perceive how handicapped they are, by laws which prevent their election to town and county councils, and debar them from the parliamentary suffrage. It is not only because women's own particular interests suffer, that they demand that such indignities should cease. The nation cannot afford to sacrifice anything in the battle for a juster life. It must inevitably suffer if it leaves more than half the community on one side, undeveloped and unrepresented; it cannot afford to dispense with the help which women can bring.

Nor, as long as Guild members remain willing to learn, need they fear their own inexperience. The Guild is, their training ground—their own organisation, to use in the ways which will be of the greatest service to themselves and others.

It is not only the individual who has been made conscious, through the Guild, of latent power, but a new element is entering into public life. Working-women form the largest section of the community. Four million women and girls are actual wealth-producers, receiving payment for their work. Still larger in numbers are the married women, who, as home-makers, contribute by their unpaid labour just as directly as wage-earners to the support of family life. This class is now, through organisation, finding its voice, formulating its needs, and taking its part in administrative work as Co-operators and citizens.

APPENDICES.

I.

MEMBERS OF THE CENTRAL COMMITTEE.

Mrs. ACLAND—Secretary, 1883; President, 1884 to 1886.

Mrs. LAWRENSON—1884 to 1892; General Secretary, 1885 to 1889.

Miss ALLEN (Mrs. Redfearn)—1884 to 1888; General Secretary, 1884.

Miss GREENWOOD—1884 to 1886; 1888.

Mrs. HELLIWELL—1884.

Mrs. B. JONES—1884 to 1892; 1898; President, 1886 to 1892.

Miss SHUFFLEBOTHAM (Mrs. Trotman)—1884 to 1891.

Miss WEBB—1885 to 1888; 1892; 1898.

Mrs. HILL—1885; 1886.

Miss SHARP—1886 to 1891.

Mrs. CARTER—1887 to 1890.

Miss LLEWELYN DAVIES—1888; General Secretary, 1889 to present time.

Miss HOLYOAKE (Mrs. Holyoake-Marsh)—1888 to 1891; 1898.

Miss REDDISH—1889 to 1891; 1895 to 1898; President, 1897.

Miss TOURNIER—1890 to 1892; 1894; 1895; President, 1892.

Miss SPOONER—1891 to 1893; 1896.

Mrs. KNOTT—1892; 1898.

Mrs. ASHWORTH—1892 to 1894; 1897; 1898; President, 1898; 1894.

Mrs. ADAMS—1894 to 1896; President, 1895.

Mrs. BURY—1894 to 1896; 1898 to 1900; 1902 to present time;
  President, 1896..

Mrs. SPENCE—1894; 1895.

Mrs. HODGETT—1895 to 1897; 1899 to 1901; President, 1900.

Mrs. CARR—1896 to 1898; President, 1898.

Mrs. DEANS—1897 to 1899; President, 1899.

Mrs. WIDLAKE—1897 to 1899.

Mrs. DRING—1898.

Mrs. BOOTHMAN—1899 to 1901; President, 1901.

Mrs. POTTER—1899.

Mrs. BENTLEY—1900; 1901.

Mrs. GREEN—1900 to present time; President, 1902.

Mrs. MC.BLAIN—1900 to present time; President, 1903.

Mrs. BUTTERFIELD—1901 to present time.

Mrs. FIDKIN—1902 to present time.

Mrs. NIGHTINGALE—1902 to present time.

II.

SECTIONAL SECRETARIES.

Midland Section.— Miss MC.GOWAN—1889; 1890. Miss SHUFFLE-
  BOTHAM—1891. Miss SPOONER—1892; 1893; 1894. Mrs.
  HODGETT—1895 to 1897; 1899. Mrs. VANN—1898. Mrs.
  SIMONS—1900 to 1902. Mrs. HALL—1903 to present time.

Northern Section. —Miss HODGSON—1892. Mrs. SPENCE—1893;
  1894. Mrs. CARR—1895 to 1900. Mrs. SMITH—1901 to
  present time.

North-Western Section.—Mrs. BROWN—1890. Miss L. HARRIS—
  1891 to 1893. Miss BAMFORD (Mrs. Tomlinson)—1894 to
  present time.

Southern Section.—Miss TOURNIER—1889; 1890. Miss SPOONER—
  1891 to present time.

Western and South-Western Section.—Mrs. ADAMS—1890 to 1898.
  · · Mrs. HARTNOLL—1899 to 1901. Mrs. HUTTON—1902 to
  present time.

III.

The following table gives the progress of the Guild from 1890, when the annual publication of the number of branches and membership was begun :—

	1890	1891.	1892.	1893.	1894.
Number of Branches ..	58	64	98	137	171
Number of Members ..	1402	2406	4087	6412	7511

	1895.	1896.	1897.	1898.	1899.
Number of Branches ..	182	200	223	237	262
Number of Members ..	8004	9093	10555	12108	12587

	1900.	1901.	1902.	1903.	1904.
Number of Branches ..	278	294	298	322	359
Number of Members ..	12909	18278	14186	16140	18556

IV.

ANNUAL MEETINGS AND CONGRESSES.

SUBJECTS.

1885.—At Oldham Co-operative Congress.
    (1) Guild Children.
    (2) Representation of the Guild at Congress.
1886.—At Plymouth Co-operative Congress.
    (1) Guild Organisation.
    (2) Drapery Departments.
1887.—At Carlisle Co-operative Congress.
    (1) Formation of a Southern District Committee.
    (2) Co-operative Association for Needlewomen and Work Girls.
    (3) Guild Dividends.
1888.—At Dewsbury Co-operative Congress.
    Branch Work of the Women's Co-operative Guild.
1889.—At Ipswich Co-operative Congress.
    Further Organisation of the Guild.

1890.—At Glasgow Co-operative Congress.
>Addresses by Mr. Maxwell (S.C.W.S.) and the late Mrs. Lindsay (Glasgow).

1891.—At Lincoln Co-operative Congress.
>Addresses by Mrs. Cracroft (Lincoln) and Mr. Scotton (Derby).

1892.—At Rochdale Co-operative Congress.
>Addresses by Miss E. C. Wilson (Manchester) and Mr. Young (Plymouth).

1893.—Leicester (First Guild Annual Meeting held separately from the Co-operative Congress).
>(1) Women as Shareholders and Officials in the Co-operative Movement.
>(2) Co-operation as applied to Domestic Life.

1894.—Doncaster.
>(1) The Guild and the Local Government Act.
>(2) The Factory Bill.
>(3) Guild Organisation in Large Towns.
>(4) Conditions of Membership as affecting Women.
>(5) Guild Entertainments.
>(6) Branch Reports in "Woman's Corner."

1895.—London.
>(1) Half-time System.
>(2) Suggested Reforms in Co-operative Education.

1896.—Burnley.
>(1) Report of Investigations into Women's Work.
>(2) Preliminary Report of Inquiry into conditions of Work of Women's Co-operative Employés.
>(3) Woman Membership and Surplus Capital.

1897.—Sunderland.
>(1) Accidents Compensation Act.
>(2) High Dividends.
>(3) Poor Law Questions.

1898.—Derby.
>(1) Co-operative House-Building.
>(2) Co-operative Productions.

1899.—Plymouth.
>(1) Women on Management Committees.
>(2) Women on Educational Committees.
>(3) First Years of Childhood.

1900.—Woolwich.
    (1) A Co-operative Relief Column.
    (2) Housing.
    (8) District Work.
    (4) Factory Legislation.
    (5) Women and Local Government.

1901.—Blackpool.
    (1) Temperance Reform from a National Standpoint.
    (2) Co-operative Life Insurance.

1902.—Newcastle.
    (1) Report of Inquiry on Co-operation and the Poor.
    (2) Desirability of Open Membership.

1908.—Lincoln.
    (1) The Co-operative Wholesale Society from the Guild Standpoint.
    (2) Women and County and Borough Councils.

V.

SECTIONAL CONFERENCES.

SUBJECTS.

1889.—N.W. Section: Guild Work.
    S. Section: Work of Sectional and District Sections.

1890.—N.W. and S. Sections: Co-operative Orphanage.
                             Guild Work.

1891.—M. and W. Sections: Guild Work.
    N.W. and S. Sections: Co-operative Workshops.

1892.—All Sections: Winter Circular.

1898.—N.W. Section: Guild Organisation.
    M., N., and N.W. Sections: Winter Circular and New Rules.
                                  Guild Work.
    S. Section: Winter Circular and New Rules.
                Factory and Workshops Acts.
    W. Section: Guild Work.

1894.—All Sections: Conditions of Shop Assistants, &c., outside
                      the Co-operative Movement.

1895.—Spring: Women and Local Government.
    Autumn: Machinery of Co-operative Movement.

1896.—Spring: Organisation of the Guild.
        Autumn : Characteristic Working Days in (a) the Home,
              (b) the School, (c) the Mill, (d) the Store,
              (e) the Dressmaker's Workshop.

1897.—Spring: Machinery Accidents (N.W. Section).
              Why Working Women need the Vote (M., N., S.,
                and W. Sections).
        Autumn : Winter Circular.
              Public Health.

1898.—Spring: Guild Work in relation to Educational Committees.
        Autumn : Credit and High Prices.

1899.—Spring : Emergency Funds.
        Autumn : Co-operation in Poor Neighbourhoods.

1900.—Spring : Cooked Meat Shops (N.W. and S.).
              Loan Departments (M. and N.).
              A People's Store (W. and S.W.).
        Autumn : General, District, and Branch Rules.

1901.—Spring : Old Age Pensions.
        Autumn : The People's Claim on the Land.

1902.—Spring : The Co-operative Store (Part I.).
        Autumn: The Open Door (N. and S. and Special N.W.
                Conference joint with Co-operative Union).
              National Education and Popular Control (N.W.
                and M.).
              Co-operation and the Poor (W. and S.W. joint
                with Co-operative Union).

1903.—Spring : Co-operative Houses to Own or to Rent (M., N.,
              N.W., and W. and S.W.).
              Wage-earning Children (S.).
        Autumn : Necessity for Free Trade.

Printed and Bound at the
Co-operative Wholesale Society's Printing Works,
Hamilton Road, Longsight,
Manchester.

Lightning Source UK Ltd.
Milton Keynes UK
UKHW020628190721
387400UK00004B/202